# MYTHS AND MYSTERIES

## OF

# PENNSYLVANIA

### TRUE STORIES
### OF THE UNSOLVED AND UNEXPLAINED

## KARA HUGHES

Guilford, Connecticut

*To my parents, who have braved many things*
*(including Centralia) with me*

Copyright © 2012 by Morris Book Publishing, LLC

Maps by Melissa Baker © Morris Book Publishing, LLC
Layout: Maggie Peterson
Project editor: Lynn Zelem

Library of Congress Cataloging-in-Publication Data

Hughes, Kara.
  Myths and mysteries of Pennsylvania : true stories of the unsolved and unexplained / Kara Hughes. — First edition.
    pages cm. — (Myths and mysteries series)
  Includes bibliographical references and index.
  ISBN 978-0-7627-7229-2
  1. Pennsylvania—History—Anecdotes. 2. Pennsylvania—Social life and customs—Anecdotes. 3. Curiosities and
wonders—Pennsylvania—Anecdotes. 4. Pennsylvania—History, Local—Anecdotes. 5. Pennsylvania—Biography—Anecdotes. I. Title.
  F149.6.H84 2012
  974.8—dc23

                                                    2012030450

Printed in the United States of America

10 9 8 7 6 5 4 3 2 1

# CONTENTS

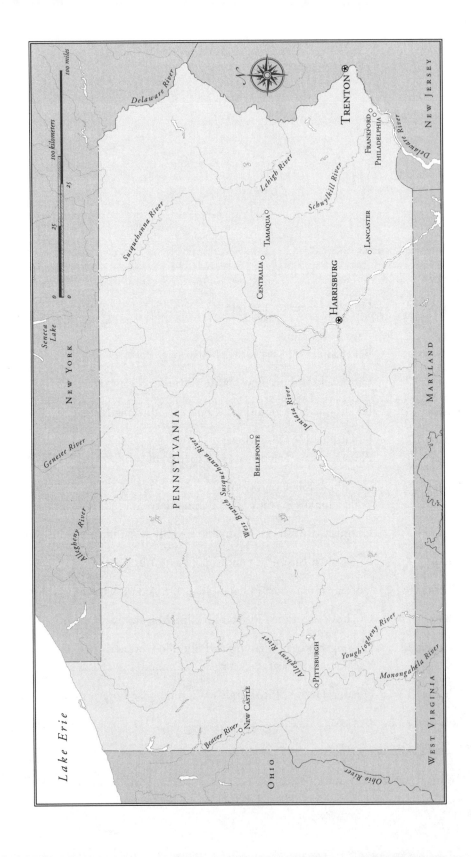

# ACKNOWLEDGMENTS

Meredith Rufino, for thoughtfully securing this project for me

Erin Turner (again!), for her insight and patience, patience, patience

Research librarians, authors, historians, and blog-keepers, for being incredibly helpful even though I was a mere stranger who insisted on communicating using only lower-case letters

Coworkers, who somehow knew when to steer clear and when to celebrate

Friends, for asking and encouraging and, when necessary, distracting

Bergen Street, for hosting both furious typing and prolonged plotting

My two favorite people from the state of Maine, for coming to me and heading off what felt like crisis

ACKNOWLEDGMENTS

Cate, Jared, and Eoin, my trifecta of all that is good

"Warm Hearts," the soundtrack of this project

And Pittsburgh, for giving me some of my favorite faces, places, and pastimes, and for serving as my introduction to the great state of Pennsylvania

# PREFACE

I don't know exactly when my grandmother started believing in ghosts. It was certainly after my grandfather had died, when she was living alone for the first time in her life. Early on, the stories teetered between noteworthy and eerie: She'd wake up to a figure standing at the foot of her bed, or she'd round a corner just in time to see something dart out of sight. But, as she grew older, the visions became more permanent fixtures in her home.

Of her cadre of ghosts, there were two who were my favorites. First, was the ghost of a man who my gramma insisted lived in a ceiling air vent. The man, she explained, was a doctor whose primary trade was making wooden legs for babies. My grandmother spoke with admiration about his job, although she admitted that the doctor was so busy that he didn't pay her too many visits. Her most frequent guest was a young girl who was completely mute and always getting into trouble. The way my gramma would tell it, this little girl would overturn pillows, break certain items, and hide others. And, whenever it seemed like she might get in trouble, the girl would dash from the room. Every so often, the little girl would make an appearance when I was present, causing my gramma's eyes to wet with a discernible tenderness. I didn't have to see the girl to understand how much my grandmother believed in her.

The girl provided my grandmother with company and, at times, entertainment. Her presence also afforded my gramma the opportunity to feel like a caregiver—a role that she played for most of her life. When talking to my grandmother about her visions, I often found myself ignoring the legitimacy of the ghosts, instead preferring to celebrate the fact that they seemed to add something different—something good—to my gramma's days.

Here are two things that I'm neglecting to mention: At the time she was seeing these figures, my grandmother had glaucoma and Alzheimer's. The glaucoma had grown worse as she aged, and near the end of her life, she was seeing in swirls as opposed to pixels. As for her dementia, she used to equate it to the sound of wood breaking in her brain, where her memories and thoughts were splintering without her being able to stop the destruction. In speaking with a doctor friend about her visions, I learned that the little girl my grandmother saw was likely her own reflection. Apparently this is a relatively common occurrence among people with dementia, whose brains are scrambling to attach meaning to things as the world makes less and less sense. My gramma was, in essence, a mystery maker.

Mysteries, at their very heart, exist alongside illogical situations, happenstances, and events. Sometimes we don't want to arm ourselves with enough information to actually solve what is so puzzling—we want, actually, to preserve the mystery. Other times, the mystery itself is less engaging than untangling the mess that created it.

Rooted in oral tradition, mysteries need an audience. My gramma's living with ghosts was not necessarily perplexing to her, and instead only became mysterious when she shared it with those of us who did not share her reality. When a mystery is told over and over, it is grows into a myth. The relationship between mysteries and myths is one of origin and progeny. Essentially, myths are born out of mysteries that are worth telling again and again, which leads us to Pennsylvania and the stories that follow.

Accounting for Pennsylvania's 46,058 square miles, we visit seven different counties, spending time inside of prisons and mines, working alongside of innovators and vigilantes, and chasing unidentified killers and murderers. Whether these myths are real or imagined, unfortunate, secretive, or legendary, they have become embedded into the culture, history, and geography of the state. Welcome to tales of Pennsylvania's Unsolved Crimes, Unfathomable Conditions, Unfinished Business, Unclear Intentions, and Unsung Heroes.

# CHAPTER 1

## *Unsolved Crimes: Frankford's Slasher*

In the city, asphalt boils as summer temperatures keep pace with the rising sun; the heat intensifies with hurried bodies in motion. On the morning of August 26, 1985, two Southeastern Pennsylvania transportation authority workers reported to the yard of the Frankford, Pennsylvania, elevated train, likely bracing for the heat of the day. What they found would make them stop dead on the tracks.

Splayed across the railroad tiles was the body of Helen Patent, wearing nothing from the waist down. The fifty-two-year-old's legs were outstretched and pried open; her shirt was pulled up so that her breasts were exposed. Slashed and stabbed forty-seven times, Patent's head and chest were littered with knife marks, the deepest of which stretched across her stomach causing her body to spill out onto itself. It was later discovered that she had been sexually assaulted prior to her death.

Within a day, police had pieced together Ms. Patent's history. Her official residence was with her ex-husband in Parkland,

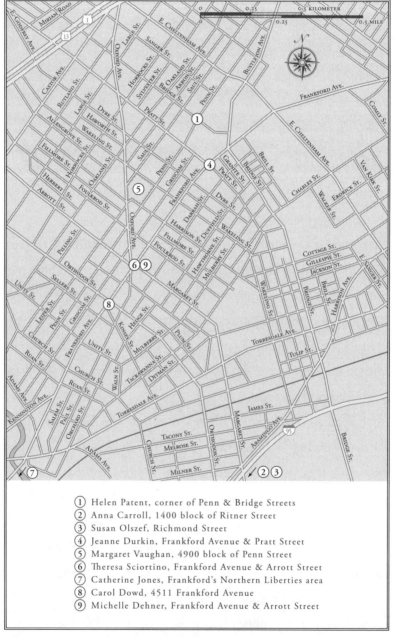

1. Helen Patent, corner of Penn & Bridge Streets
2. Anna Carroll, 1400 block of Ritner Street
3. Susan Olszef, Richmond Street
4. Jeanne Durkin, Frankford Avenue & Pratt Street
5. Margaret Vaughan, 4900 block of Penn Street
6. Theresa Sciortino, Frankford Avenue & Arrott Street
7. Catherine Jones, Frankford's Northern Liberties area
8. Carol Dowd, 4511 Frankford Avenue
9. Michelle Dehner, Frankford Avenue & Arrott Street

**FRANKFORD SLASHER VICTIMS**

A map highlighting the locations where the nine Slasher victims were discovered.

Pennsylvania, some eleven miles northwest of Frankford, although Kermit Patent didn't indicate that they spent much time together there. In fact, police found that most believed that Helen was a full-time resident of Frankford (a town located eight miles northeast of Philadelphia), as she was a familiar face at its local bars. Police were able to rule out Helen's husband as a suspect in the gruesome murder. The investigation hit a quick standstill; not only did the authorities have no suspect, but they had no form of perceivable motive for the crime. During the summer of 1985, it was too early for anyone to know that, with the discovery of Patent's body, Pennsylvania had just been introduced to one of its most dogged and violent serial killers.

Frankford certainly had prouder moments in its history, according to resident Duane Swierczynski, who described its origins: "First settled by Swedes in the 1660s, this tiny village became known for its main road, King's Highway, which served as the primary route between Philadelphia and New York. Horse-drawn carriages transported members of the Continental Congress in pre-Revolutionary days, and the Jolly Post Inn served as a popular way station. Washington did indeed sleep here, and legend has it that the Jolly Post was where some revolutionaries decided that Thomas Jefferson would be the one to draft the Declaration of Independence."

In more recent times, the city arguably hit its highest economic boom when construction began on the Market-Frankford El (elevated train), which opened to the public in 1922. Two years after this, the Frankford Yellow Jackets, a well-known group of footballers who were popular in the neighborhood, were granted acceptance into the newly formed National Football League. The boon was somewhat short-lived, however. By 1931 the Yellow Jackets had become homeless thanks to financial pressures and a fire that destroyed their stadium (though they reemerged in the League in 1933 under their present name, the Philadelphia Eagles). After Frankford lost this great source of hometown pride, the city muddled through the mid-twentieth century, keeping afloat without triumph or tragedy. If you ask locals, they'd tell you that depravity didn't really strike until the 1980s, when the town's once-thriving commercial district had become fully burdened with crime and destitution.

During the Reagan years, Frankford's alleyways played host to prostitutes and junkies, who knew that, after six o'clock, foot traffic was isolated to those spilling out of the Golden Bar or the Happy Tap, too blind with drink to care much about legalities. The clanging hum generated by the rusted El did little to deter any criminal activity, so tricks were turned and crack smoked with the permission granted by near anonymity. At that time, the bottomed-out feel of Frankford's streets was palpable enough to prompt Sylvester Stallone to film his *Rocky* movies in and along Frankford Avenue. Even still, up until the summer of 1985, it seemed like life in town was regulated by a manageable arrangement: Professionals ran their businesses during daylight hours, and by nightfall the streets were turned over to the night crews, who kept within their own circles. Everything was copa-cetic until Helen Patent's body was found under the El. On that August morning, this northeast Philadelphia neighborhood rattled awake to a new scourge: murder.

The killer, who would later earn the title of the Frank-ford Slasher, waited just over four months to strike again. The Slasher's second victim, discovered on January 3, 1986, was sixty-eight-year-old Anna Carroll. Carroll was found lying in the bedroom of her Ritner Street apartment, naked from the waist-down, having suffered from six stab wounds, one of which stretched from her breast to her pubic bone. There was no mis-taking what the assailant used as a weapon, as the kitchen knife used to kill Carroll was found inside of her body.

Police only released scant information about Carroll's life-style and habits: All anyone seemed willing to confirm is that she, like Helen Patent, was a known Frankford barfly. No wit-nesses were identified in either crime. As was the case with their investigation into Patent's murder, the police could not deter-mine any discernible motive that might have driven someone to kill Anna Carroll.

Although Philadelphia police acknowledged that there were comparisons between Helen Patent's death and the mur-der of Anna Carroll, they were apparently unwilling to link the investigations or raise suspicion that a repeat offender might be walking the streets of Frankford. It's relevant to note that testing crime scenes for DNA was not an option at that time.

In the twenty-first century we take DNA evidence for granted, knowing that locations and victims can be swabbed and matters analyzed to expedite police work. But, in the eighties, the Philadelphia police had no such luxury. DNA testing did not even come to be until 1985, while the first criminal conviction based on DNA evidence was not made until 1987. Even still, analyzing DNA did not become a common police tactic until well into the 1990s.

With so little evidence with which to work, the investigation hit wall after wall. Meanwhile, the Slasher remained quiet. His third victim was not discovered until Christmas Day, 1986, nearly one year after Carroll's murder. Susan Olszef, a sixty-four-year-old, was found in her Richmond Street apartment, only three miles from where Helen Patent's body had been discovered. Like the others before her, Olszef was a familiar sight at the Golden Bar (known as "Goldie's" to locals), but her profession, hobbies, and interests were all relatively unknown.

While the investigation into Olszef's death was still fresh, the Slasher struck again, this time attacking a much younger victim. Twenty-eight-year-old Jeanne Durkin was found on January 8, 1987, laid out beneath a storage truck parked on Pratt Street. Durkin's body was situated just a few lots over from Goldie's bar and only one block from where Helen Patent was murdered. In what was becoming recognized as his signature fashion, the Slasher had stripped Jeanne from the waist down, positioning her legs so that she was found with them spread wide open. The young woman was stabbed seventy-four times; the heinous brutality of the attack was marked by blood splatters covering the truck and surrounding scene. Tests later revealed that she had been sexually assaulted prior to her death.

Unlike the killer's previous victims, Jeanne Durkin had a recognized life outside of frequenting Goldie's each night. Durkin, who was homeless, was a familiar face to anyone who spent time in and around the neighborhood's commercial district, especially patrons of a local bakery in whose doorway she regularly slept.

By 1987, there was no longer any doubt that the town was playing host to a serial killer who made victims of women who were down on their luck. With the January death of Jeanne Durkin, the *Philadelphia Inquirer* began pressuring the police department to devote more of its resources to identifying and capturing Frankford's murderer. It wasn't like the police weren't taking the crime spree seriously; it was more like they had their hands full. Unbelievably, in the late 1980s the Frankford Slasher's crimes were not even the most repugnant crimes the city had witnessed.

Leading up to 1990, Philadelphia was experiencing an outburst of violent crimes against women. In March 1987, Josefina Rivera, a runaway-turned-prostitute, called the police, claiming that she had escaped a house where a man was holding her and roughly five other women hostage. The man turned out to be Gary Heidnik, described by journalist Brian Hickey as "a forty-three-year-old high school dropout and self-ordained minister who had a knack for making money in the stock market and a history of sexual abuse and mental problems." Police were horrified to learn that Heidnik had at one time kept six women under the age of twenty-five, at least one of whom was mentally challenged, chained up in his basement. At the time of his arrest, only Rivera and three others were still living.

Through victim statements, Heidnik came alive as a true sadist. Sometimes his prisoners were thrown into a hole he had dug in his basement; sometimes they were chained, nearly naked, to sewage pipes. Sometimes Heidnik raped them; sometimes they had to watch as he raped others. Worried that the women would scream for help, Heidnik played a radio constantly, and was also in the habit of ramming a screwdriver into the ears of his victims until he saw blood. When one woman died from asphyxiation, Heidnik removed her from the basement, used an electric knife to cut her into pieces, and served her flesh to the others the following day. Heidnik forced his first hostage, Josefina Rivera, to electrocute another woman after that victim proved "uncooperative." After his arrest, Heidnik stood trial on over ten charges, and received the death penalty: He died of lethal injection in July 1999.

As if Philadelphia wasn't already plagued by the visions Heidnik's "Horror House" provided, five months after his March 1987 arrest, the city was introduced to another serial killer: Harrison "Marty" Graham. On August 7, Graham had been evicted from his flophouse apartment due to an offensive odor coming from his residence. When the landlord sent his own son to clean out Graham's flat, it was discovered that, in addition to piles of rotting feces and waist-high mounds of trash, the apartment contained a locked door. Through an open keyhole, the unmoving, naked legs of a woman could be seen. The landlord's son contacted the Philadelphia police, and within hours police found four dead women inside of the locked room.

Initially investigators believed that the bodies belonged to drug addicts who had simply crawled into the room to expire. However, Marty Graham's involvement in the women's deaths became more and more certain after police began to find corpses that were mummified, thanks to their having been purposefully wrapped in layers of thin blankets and stacked on top of one another. Eventually, a total of seven female corpses, in various states of decay, were discovered behind Graham's locked door. As opposed to the case of Gary Heidnik, who was in custody at the time police became privy to his hideous transgressions, this case was not so easily concluded. Marty Graham's whereabouts were unknown.

When police questioned the men who evicted Graham, they learned that he left in a hurry, and with very few possessions. Journalist Katherine Ramsland noted that "he was wearing white pants, a striped jacket, and a cap, and he had his raggedy blue Cookie Monster [puppet with him]." Graham, who had been diagnosed with a severe learning disability as a child, was on the lam for one week, evading police (perhaps unknowingly) by crashing in various Philly flophouses and drug dens. Ten days later, Marty's mother convinced him to surrender to the police. While initially he told officials that the corpses had "been there when [he] moved in," under questioning he later admitted to strangling all seven victims. He stated that all of the murders were effected during sex and while he was under the influence of drugs. After being declared competent to stand trial, Marty Graham was ultimately sentenced to life in prison.

Between Heidnik and Graham, the pages of Philadelphia papers were overflowing with gory, albeit gripping, details of local crime. It is perhaps because Philadelphia citizens were primed with this relentless insight into criminal behaviors that pressure on city police to find the Frankford Slasher heightened. Knowing what Heidnik and Graham were capable of made not knowing what the Slasher looked like, or what he was after, that much more terrifying.

In August 1987 the police department formed a task force to canvass the areas where the Slasher's victims were found. The efforts were somewhat successful. Between Goldie's customers and bartenders, police were getting a better idea of the temperaments of the Slasher's victims, Helen Patent and Jeanne Durkin in particular. Folks who had regular interaction with the women detailed their belief that Patent and Durkin would not have been taken advantage of easily, leading police to suspect that the Slasher knew his victims.

On November 10, 1988, two students who lived in an apartment building on Penn Street discovered the Slasher's next victim, sixty-six-year-old Margaret Vaughan. Vaughan had apparently been evicted from her residence earlier that day, for failure to pay rent; her body was found in an inner vestibule of the building. Vaughan had been stabbed twenty-nine times, suffering from wounds about her torso, head, and neck; testing later revealed that she had not been sexually assaulted prior to (or following) her death. Vaughan had two hundred dollars on her person at the time of her murder. Lieutenant James Henwood of the Philadelphia Police Department's Homicide Unit remarked to the *Philadelphia Inquirer* that the department was "stuck for a motive."

Unsurprisingly, the police went back to the Frankford Avenue bars to question staff or patrons, hoping that someone had information about Vaughan or her potential killer. As journalist Katherine Ramsland detailed, "A barmaid recalled that Vaughan had been in the bar the evening before her death with a Caucasian man with a round face who walked with a limp and wore glasses." The police created a sketch with assistance from the bartender. But, despite the fact that the suspected killer's likeness had been distributed throughout Frankford, no witnesses came forward, and the Frankford Slasher continued to walk the streets unrecognized.

The body of the Slasher's sixth victim, Theresa Sciortino, was found on January 19, 1989. The thirty-year-old's body was discovered in her Arrott Street apartment, three blocks from

Margaret Vaughan's residence. The scene in Sciortino's kitchen was macabre: Her body, which was clad only in white socks, was lying face-up in a dark pool of blood. The knife the killer used to slash her face, arms, and chest some twenty-five times was left in the kitchen sink. A three-foot-long piece of wood was also found in the kitchen, which police later determined had been used to sexually assault the victim.

Upon questioning, Sciortino's neighbors admitted that they had heard a struggle the previous night, including a "loud thump." The crime scene evidenced that Sciortino made efforts to ward off her attacker: Bloodstains were found throughout her apartment.

In addition to the fact that she lived near other Slasher victims, Sciortino shared other things in common with some of her fellow victims: She was a regular at the Frankford Avenue bars, she had a history of being in and out of mental institutions, and she was often seen in the company of men—leading some to believe that she might have been an occasional prostitute. Police determined that on the night of her murder, Theresa had been at the Jolly Post Tavern, leaving around six o'clock with a man described as middle-aged and white.

Lieutenant Henwood told reporters that the police were considering Sciortino's death the work of a serial killer. The facts seemed indisputable: The victims were white women, most of whom lived in the same area of town, most of whom were barflies, and all of whom had been stabbed to death. In culling through evidence from other unsolved crimes in and around

Frankford, police discovered that the Slasher might also have killed twenty-nine-year-old Catherine Jones, whose body had been found in January 1987. As was common with victims of the Slasher, Jones was a regular at the Frankford Avenue pubs, and her body was discovered only partially clothed. However, police held some skepticism that Jones had died at the hands of the Slasher, as her body was not stabbed; instead, she had been bludgeoned to death.

As if to toy with Philadelphia police, who felt an urgent need now to capture and punish the Slasher, the murderer lay quiet for some fifteen months following the January 1989 death of Theresa Sciortino. Then, on April 29, 1990, a patrol officer discovered the naked body of forty-six-year-old Carol Dowd, just behind a seafood store located on Frankford Avenue. The condition of Dowd's body was gruesome: she had been stabbed thirty-six times about her face, neck, chest, and back; she had defensive wounds on her hands; her left nipple had been removed; and her stomach was open with a deep wound exposing her intestines.

An unidentified witness told police that, during the evening of the murder, she had seen Dowd walking alongside of a white man not far from the crime scene: The Frankford Slasher, it seemed, had struck again. And yet, the man who began to garner police interest was not the round-faced, bespectacled white man who had been placed alongside two of the Slasher's victims on the day of their deaths. Instead, the investigation into Dowd's death was intently focused on Leonard Christopher, an

African-American employed at the fish market behind which Dowd's body was discovered.

Christopher first raised investigators' suspicions when, during discussion with police, he volunteered that he had known Margaret Vaughan, the Slasher's fifth victim. Christopher wound up in deeper trouble when his girlfriend did not corroborate his alibi that he had spent the night of Dowd's murder with her. Following this, police located a witness who placed Leonard Christopher at the same bar Dowd had been seen at on the night that she was killed. As if all of this wasn't damning enough, a prostitute who had earlier told police that she knew nothing of Dowd's whereabouts on April 29, changed her story. She not only said that she had seen Dowd and Christopher together in a bar, but she also claimed to have later seen Christopher by himself walking out of the alley located behind the fish shop. According to this eyewitness, Christopher was "sweating and had a large knife in his belt." When police later searched Christopher's apartment and found bloody clothes there, they did not buy his explanation that his boss at the seafood market had asked him to clean up blood in the alley. Jaesa Phang, Christopher's boss at the fish market, later told police that, during a private conversation, Christopher had suggested, "Maybe I killed her," an assertion that he apparently quickly recanted. Despite the tenuous nature of the witness's accounts, on May 5, Leonard Christopher was charged with possession of a criminal weapon, robbery, murder, and abuse of a corpse.

Christopher, who was held without bail, was in prison when the Slasher's final victim, thirty-year-old Michelle Dehner, also known as Michelle Martin, was found dead in an Arrott Street apartment. Dehner, who lived on the same block as victim Theresa Sciortino, and three blocks from where Carol Dowd's body had been found, was stabbed twenty-three times by her assailant. According to the *Philadelphia Inquirer,* Dehner was known about the Frankford neighborhood as "Crazy Michelle," a "hard-drinking, paranoid loner." Witnesses attested to having seen Dehner at a local watering hole with a white man a day or two before her body was discovered.

Although Leonard Christopher did not fit the description of the man last seen with Margaret Vaughn, Theresea Sciortino, or Michelle Dehner, thus suggesting that he was not the man responsible for any of the Frankford Slasher deaths, he stood trial for Carol Dowd's murder. On December 12, 1990, Christopher was found guilty of the first-degree murder of Dowd. It is perhaps unsurprising that Christopher, who, at the time of this publication, remains incarcerated at SCI Huntingdon, maintains his innocence. He believes that he was the victim of police pressure to solve the Slasher case, and has asserted that prostitutes "pipered" by giving authorities false testimony in order to convict him.

While many held serious doubts that Christopher was responsible for Carol Dowd's murder, no one believed that he was responsible for all of the Slasher's murders. But, when no other victims were found after Crazy Michelle, clamor about the Frankford Slasher died down. Theories were thrown about, including the belief that there was no Slasher at all, but rather just a murder followed by a series of copycat killings. In practice, the cold cases took a back seat to more pressing investigations.

In 2010, a CBS Channel 3 report by Walt Hunter revealed that the Philadelphia Police Department did not fully shelve the investigations and was still pursuing the case using new DNA technology to try to identify the Frankford Slasher. Since Michelle Dehner's death in 1990, according to Hunter, police have theorized that the Slasher might have "posed as a counselor offering guidance and consolation, [possibly] even renting an office in a nearby church." It is thought that the Slasher would meet and get to know his victims in bars, earning their trust over a period of time. Hunter reported that police had a "prime suspect" whose relocation out of Pennsylvania coincided with the end of the Slasher's murders. However, according to Hunter, this "prime suspect" died in 2008 and police are unwilling to name him as the possible Slasher without confirmed DNA evidence. As of the date of this publication, the Frankford Slasher remains the only serial killer in Philadelphia's history never to have been caught or captured.

# CHAPTER 2

## Unsolved Crimes: Bellefonte's Missing District Attorney, Ray Gricar

April 15: If you're an American, you might shudder at the date. Tax day can stir up a lot of concern—whether you're worried that you didn't file properly, don't have the funds to cover what you owe, or maybe you're not even close to being ready to submit all that's necessary to the IRS. On April 15, 2005, Ray Gricar, the District Attorney for Pennsylvania's Centre County, expressed no such concern. According to his live-in girlfriend, Patty Fornicola, when he woke up on the fifteenth, Ray casually announced that he was going to play hooky for the day. He had done it before. He was eight months away from retirement and had already started to ease out from under his workload; no one was going to argue that he didn't deserve a day off. As Patty left to report to the DA's office where she was employed as a clerk, Ray remained in the house, apparently undecided about how he wanted to spend the day. They likely kissed goodbye, treating their parting as nothing beyond ordinary, temporary. But in leaving their Bellefonte, Pennsylvania home, Patty Fornicola became the last known person to see Ray Gricar, dead or alive.

Ray Frank Gricar was born in Collinwood, Ohio, on October 9, 1945. Collinwood, a predominately Polish neighborhood located on the east side of Cleveland, was a very easy place to foster a devotion to the hometown Cleveland Indians. When Ray was three and his older brother Roy was five, the Indians won the World Series. The Gricar boys would see Cleveland play in another World Series in 1954, when the Indians were swept by the New York Giants. Despite the team's plummet into embarrassing mediocrity, Ray remained a devoted fan.

After graduating from Gilmour Academy, a Catholic prep school, Ray traveled south to Dayton, Ohio, to pursue his bachelor's degree. While there, he met Barbara Gray, the woman who would become his first wife. Although he originally intended to study Russian history, an internship with the prosecutor's office led Ray to the law. After he and Barbara graduated, they moved to Cleveland where Ray attended Case Western Reserve's Law School. With his law degree in hand, Ray began work as Cuyahoga County's assistant prosecutor.

Cleveland is not a soft city, and Ray's job gave him exposure to all sorts of crimes. It was here that he began to develop his no-nonsense style. As Robert Buehner, a DA who would later work with Ray in Pennsylvania detailed, "He was the most serious guy, most ethical guy." Another colleague said that Ray was the kind of person who would see you out of his office as a meeting was ending—he didn't engage in idle chitchat, at least not while at work. Granted, Ray might not have been the first guy you thought to invite out for beers after a long day in court, but his name and experience did promise professionalism.

The Gricar household grew when in 1978 Ray and Barbara adopted a newborn daughter; like her father, Lara spent her formative years in Cleveland. The family stayed in Ohio until 1985, when Barbara was offered a job at Penn State University. Ray embraced the move and the change it offered; once they were settled in State College, he began acting as a stay-at-home dad for Lara, who was then seven years old. Lara and Ray would always be close; even after she moved out west to Seattle for college, she regularly talked to her dad two or three times each week.

Ray's career as a househusband did not last long. It just so happens that, right around the time that the Gricars were relaxing into their new routine, Ray received a phone call from the Centre County District Attorney, David Grine. Grine was looking for an assistant and had heard good things about Ray's work in Cleveland. The job was part-time and the pace was much slower than Ray's work had been in Ohio: For as long as anyone could remember, Centre County hadn't averaged more than two homicides a year. After a bit of waffling, Ray accepted the job. And when in 1985 Grine was elected judge, Centre County residents did not hesitate to appoint Ray as his successor. Before Lara completed her first year of school in Pennsylvania,

Ray had, without even so much as trying, become the Centre County DA—a position he would hold until his disappearance some twenty years later.

Investigative journalist James Renner reports that Gricar's work did not actually turn out to be that of a slow-paced office: "In 1985, he successfully prosecuted one of the first cases in the country to use postpartum depression as a defense after a woman tossed her one-month-old son from a bridge into a local stream. She got eight to twenty years. In 1992, he prosecuted James R. Cruz, an interstate trucker who had dumped the body of a young girl on the on-ramp to I-80 heading out of town. Cruz was found guilty and sentenced to life in prison. When an ROTC student opened fire in the student union at Penn State in 1996—killing one girl and wounding another—Gricar put the shooter away for thirty to sixty years. Homicides were his specialty."

While the details of his professional life are relatively easy to account for during this time, the particulars of Ray's private life are less accessible. It is known that Ray and Barbara divorced in the early 1990s, but no data can be found as to which parent had custody of Lara and whether either of the Gricar women remained in State College after the split. Details are also hazy regarding how Ray met his second wife, Emma, whom he would marry in 1996.

Before Ray tied the knot for a second time, tragedy struck his family when his older brother Roy was reported missing. Three years older than Ray, Roy had stayed in Ohio, where he was raising his own family while working at Dayton's Wright Patterson Air Force Base. Roy was bipolar and known to battle depression; he seemed to be managing just fine until the beginning of May when he was let go at work. On one of his first days of unemployment, Roy told his wife he was going to buy mulch and never came home. His body was found on May 10 in the Great Miami River; authorities later deemed his drowning death a suicide. The news was obviously heartbreaking for Ray and members of his extended family.

By all known accounts, Ray Gricar moved forward with his life following his brother's death. He had job security in Centre County and, although his marriage to Emma ended in 2001, he found love again with Patty Fornicola, a woman he met through work. In January 2004, Ray decided not to run for reelection. He was fifty-nine years old and had served as a DA for nearly twenty years; he was admittedly ready to slip into a much-deserved retirement. Ray was incredibly fond of taking long drives. In fact, he had already started plotting the destination for his first post-retirement road trip to visit Lara in Washington state. In Patty he had a willing partner, and together they were already in the habit of frequenting antique stores surrounding their Bellefonte home. Patty would later joke that, through their antiquing, they bought a lot of plates—an item that was easy to transport and didn't threaten to clutter up the house they shared.

When Patty got a call from Ray at around eleven thirty on April 15, Ray told her of his plans to take a drive to some nearby antique shops. Patty would later tell authorities that when she asked Ray whether he was going to be home in time to let their dog out, he answered that he likely would not. It was dry and cool—fifty degrees—great weather to take Ray's red Mini Cooper out for a long drive through the Pennsylvania countryside. Plus, Ray had recently been feeling tired, and was definitely napping more than usual, so Patty figured it would be invigorating for him to have a change of scenery. She later told *Dateline NBC*'s Lester Holt that when she came home after work to discover that she had beaten Ray back to the house, she thought nothing of it and went to the gym. But Patty grew worried when Ray wasn't home in time for dinner; her concern increased when all of her calls went straight to his voicemail.

By eleven thirty that night, Patty Fornicola had called 911, explaining, "To me, it was an emergency." Of course the Bellefonte police knew exactly who the DA was, and promised Fornicola that they would put out a description of both Ray and his Mini Cooper in an attempt to locate him. According to Darrell Zaccagni, a police officer at the time, aerial photos were also ordered of the country roads surrounding the antique shops Ray was known to frequent, in an effort to determine whether he had gotten into an unreported accident en route. Zaccagni would later remark that their search was quite exhaustive. In the wake of Patty's news, the police even called Jacobs Field to alert stadium security to be on the lookout for Ray who, in the past, had skipped town only to be found in attendance at a Cleveland

Indians home game. Later, when asked whether he was alarmed over Gricar's reported disappearance, Zaccagni confirmed, "When the DA goes missing, you get a little concerned. We figured there was a much better chance foul play was involved."

The police unearthed a big lead when, on April 16, they discovered Ray's car in a Lewisburg parking lot. The red Mini was parked near "The Street of Shops," an antiques mall where, according to Patty, Ray had been before. Police were hoping that the vehicle would hold some substantial clues that would lead them to Ray. Instead, finding the car did little more than raise additional questions for investigators.

Ray's cell phone—which was powered off—was located inside the car; however, a dump of the phone's incoming and outgoing calls did not yield any suspicious or noteworthy trails. Authorities also noted an odor of tobacco in the car, as well as scant traces of ash on the passenger seat. Ray was known as being very meticulous about the condition of his car; those who were close to him could not think of a time when he ever allowed any-one to smoke inside of it. Although reports vary, there are some statements from the police that indicate the possibility that the ash was left by a smoker merely leaning into the car, lit cigarette in hand. Nevertheless, the clue was both out of the ordinary and without explanation.

What baffled police and dislodged any hope of establishing a reliable narrative to account for Ray's disappearance, was the utter lack of a crime scene. There was no sign of forced entry, no

NABIL K. MARK/*CENTRE DAILY TIMES*

Ray Gricar, March 31, 2005.

blood, no evidence of an argument, and no known eyewitnesses. To complicate matters, Lewisburg, an ordinarily quiet municipality of about twenty thousand residents, was hosting an influx of unfamiliar faces, thanks to it being Bucknell University's spring parent's weekend. Tony Gricar, Ray's nephew who had traveled from Dayton to try to aid in the search for his uncle, remarked that even he was seeing glimpses of what could have been Ray all over town. Being a middle-aged white male wearing sneakers, blue jeans, and a blue fleece certainly didn't give him cause to stand out.

Ray's car was a bit more unique, however. Police were hoping that residents would be able to speak to having seen the red Mini Cooper driving in and around town and might possibly even be able to attest to the driver's activity on April 15. But, upon further investigation, authorities determined that at least three different red Mini Coopers were spotted in Lewisburg on tax day.

Some of the Lewisburg folks were confident that the car that they saw belonged to the missing DA. Take Ivy Butterworth, who lives in Milton, five miles from Lewisburg. In 2011 she told *Dateline NBC* that she had seen Ray Gricar with a blonde woman near the Street of Shops back on April 15, 2005. According to the *Centre Daily Times,* Ms. Butterworth was jogging when she caught sight of the red Mini Cooper, a car she considered to be "cute." She added, "So I looked and saw a man, and a woman with blond hair. I remember thinking about her, 'Wow, big hair.' And I didn't think more about it . . . I never said anything to anybody because, well, what's the point? I mean, the guy was never found. If he wants to run off and go to Mexico or wherever with his girlfriend, and he's got the money to do it, hey, I wish it was me."

As the Bellefonte investigation moved to Lewisburg—Ray's last-known whereabouts—police were running into one dead end after another. As Darrell Zaccagni told journalist James Renner, "We have three or four good witnesses from down

MYTHS AND MYSTERIES OF PENNSYLVANIA

there [in Lewisburg] who are definitely ID-ing him in the park. They saw him sitting in his car, they watched him driving his Mini Cooper back and forth on Friday [April 15]. . . . We can definitely put him there on Saturday too. There's a museum right here, across from the park. I think it's called Cottingwood House. The employees watched Ray bring his car and park it two or three different times across the street. He came and left, came and left, came back. He got out of his car, sat on a bench. He was reading a newspaper or something, he just seems to have fallen off the earth."

Then, three months after his disappearance, a few men who were fishing in the Susquehanna River found what turned out to be Ray's work laptop. The computer was in terrible shape, having been wedged against a bridge and at least partially submerged in water. Notably, the hard drive had been removed, rendering the computer nearly useless from an investigative standpoint. Three months later the hard drive was recovered on a nearby riverbed; rusted and wrecked, it was in such bad condition that authorities were unable to obtain any information from it. This was a real blow to the investigation, which, by October 2005, had slowed to a near standstill. Police would later reveal that a search of Ray's home computer evidenced that someone had used the desktop to search the Internet for "how to wreck a hard drive."

Hypotheses were certainly created in an effort to explain or even dismiss Gricar's disappearance. As journalist Luke O'Brien suggested, "Strange theories proliferated. Someone claimed to have seen Gricar sitting in the Oprah studio audience. Another person snapped a photograph of a man who looked like Gricar eating at a Chili's in Nacogdoches, Texas, four months after his disappearance. The local police even agreed to work with a California psychic in the hopes of turning up a lead." In an exhaustive and at times emotional search, by the close of 2005, the Bellefonte police were left without any reliable clues to help explain what, exactly, had happened to Ray Gricar on the 15th of April.

Over time, three distinct theories regarding Ray's disappearance have emerged. There are those who believe that Ray, like his older brother, took his own life. While Ray's medical history does not reveal any documented concern that he was clinically depressed, the details of his last known hours are eerily similar to Roy's: Each man checked in with his loved one, got into his car and drove it some distance, parked it near a river, and was never seen alive again. That Ray's car was found parked near the Susquehanna is so reminiscent of Roy's death that Tony Gricar actually remembers thinking, "Here we go again," when he learned of the details surrounding his uncle's disappearance.

Another theory that has been formed is the notion that Ray purposefully walked out of his own life on April 15, 2005. Thanks to his years as a prosecutor, Ray had amassed working knowledge of criminal undertakings, and likely could have anticipated how best to cover his tracks. Authorities say that no money had been moved out of or between his accounts; however, he also might have been depositing a portion of his income into a hidden account—possibly for years—to prepare for an unannounced departure. In July 2011, this theory briefly gained momentum, when a "John Doe prisoner" (one who refused to provide his name or give any identifying information) was arrested in Utah on misdemeanor charges. The unidentified man bore a striking resemblance to an aged Ray Gricar. Within one day's time, however, it was determined that the prisoner was not the missing Centre County DA.

The remaining theory is that Ray Gricar was murdered. This line of speculation is certainly the most sensational, bringing to mind the hoards of criminals he locked up during the decades he spent in the Cuyahoga and Centre County District Attorney's offices. Had Gricar been killed, then it was likely his murderer who was responsible for removing and attempting to destroy his hard drive—a task that many who knew Ray didn't think he knew how to do on his own. But what would the district attorney of Centre County have on his work computer that could have been so damaging?

During the early fall of 2011, a story broke in State College, Pennsylvania, that resulted in not only the firing of Penn State University's president and athletic director, but also its legendary football coach, Joe Paterno. Based upon the findings of a Pennsylvania grand jury, whose graphic report was released to the press on November 5, 2011, Jerry Sandusky, a former PSU assistant coach and founder of "The Second Mile" children's charity, had "made sexual advances or sexually assaulted at least eight boys between 1994 and 2009." Details of Sandusky's alleged behavior made national news not only because it was so repulsive, but also because many Penn State officials were found to have knowledge of his misconduct and failed to do anything to stop it. Sandusky was later convicted on forty-five counts of child abuse.

Ray Gricar was the Centre County DA when, in 1998, the police were first presented with information identifying Sandusky as a pedophile. According to the mother of "Victim #6," her eleven-year-old son told her that, following an afternoon of wrestling and lifting weights with Sandusky, the former coach had made the boy shower with him. Specifically, the boy's mother told Penn State police that Sandusky had "bear-hugged" her son in the shower. With university police listening in, the mother later confronted Sandusky about the showering session. During said conversation, the former coach is reported to have remarked, "I understand. I was wrong. I wish I could get forgiveness. I know I won't get it from you. I wish I were dead." The grand jury report also reveals that the 1998 investigation into Sandusky's behavior involved the suspect being interviewed by the Pennsylvania Department of Public Welfare. During said interview, Sandusky is said to have "admitted [to] showering naked with Victim 6, admitted to hugging Victim 6 while in the shower and admitted that it was wrong."

With what appears to many as an admission of guilt, the question that begs to be asked is why Jerry Sandusky was not arrested in 1998. Looking again to the grand jury report, we learn that, "[a]fter a lengthy investigation by University Police Detective

Ronald Shreffler, the investigation was closed after then Centre County District Attorney Ray Gricar decided there would be no criminal charges." In other words, Jerry Sandusky was not prosecuted in 1998 based upon Gricar's professional discretion.

Many of Gricar's colleagues defend his 1998 decision not to pursue a case against Sandusky, recognizing that had Gricar felt that he had enough evidence to prosecute, he would have absolutely made the decision to do so. His fellow DAs are just as quick to dismiss the theory that Gricar's disappearance—or his possible death—had anything to do with his knowledge of what reportedly was going on at Penn State. According to former Montour County DA Bob Buehner, "If you're going to take somebody out in a criminal case, you go after the witnesses, you go after the people who can really get on the witness stand and do you in. . . . I see absolutely no connection between Ray Gricar's disappearance in 2005 and anything connected with Jerry Sandusky or stuff going on at Penn State."

It is possible that Ray Gricar's involvement in the Jerry Sandusky scandal is as peripheral as Mr. Buehner contends. But the fact that he was at all intertwined with the still-unfolding cover-up inarguably casts an extra shadow onto the circumstances surrounding his already mysterious disappearance.

At his daughter Lara's request, Ray Gricar was declared legally dead on July 25, 2011. His body has yet to be discovered.

# CHAPTER 3

## *Unsolved Crimes: New Castle's Murder Swamp*

Back in 1925, Pennsylvania's duck season started on September 1. If there were ducks to be hunted, you could find 'em and kill 'em, so long as your bounty didn't exceed fifteen in one day. On October 6, Samuel Hares was out alongside swampland in New Castle, a small town some fifty miles north of Pittsburgh, in search of game. The day was perfectly ordinary, and he was very alone, until he saw something odd poking out from under a log: it looked an awful lot like a human leg. It's easy to imagine how Hares's steps must have slowed, and how he likely craned his neck forward as if to get closer to the object without actually moving his base. Once he ascertained that the leg was, in fact, a leg, Samuel rushed to town to contact the police.

Detective J. M. Dunlap and Coroner J. P. Caldwell accompanied Hares back to the scene. It took them awhile to find the log and the leg because the swampland was marshy, and there were very few signifiers to help them to keep their bearings. Once the trio caught sight of the limb, Dunlap brushed away debris and leaves to expose the naked body of a headless man. The flesh appeared to be partially decomposed but, strangely, the earth that had been used to cover the body was fresh and the leaves crisp. Although a head was found a few days later—buried at the opposite end of the log—having the complete body didn't give the county police any better leads in identifying the male victim.

News of the headless corpse was unsettling. While common wisdom wanted to excuse the murder as an anomaly, when two hunters found a second body on October 17, and that cadaver was also headless, it became acceptable to feel worried. The second body was more skeletal than the first, and wearing both a shirt (blue) and pants (tan), but it was decapitated, and it led to something that was unlike anything locals had ever encountered. As historian Thomas White describes, "While volunteers looked for the second man's skull, which was ultimately found about two hundred yards away, a third skull was found." After J. P. Caldwell's close examination, it was determined that this third skull had likely been submerged in swampland for some twelve months. And, unlike the other two skulls, this one belonged to a female. Eventually, bits and pieces of a fourth victim (a male) were also discovered in the vicinity.

Thinking back to the last year, and even the last few years, police were forced to acknowledge that there had been two other victims found in or around New Castle's swampland who had suffered some form of mutilation. Emma Jackson, an older West Pittsburgh resident, had been discovered dead inside her home in 1921. While there was no sign of forced entry and no apparent robbery, the condition of Jackson's body was gruesome, as her head was connected to her body by just a few tendons. In addition to Jackson's death, there was also the severed torso of a girl that was discovered in 1923, floating in a river running alongside of the swamp.

Although there were some notable similarities between these crimes—namely, the dismemberment of victims' bodies—county police also knew that the desolate, sinking marshland of New Castle had long been a prime area for local gang members and mobsters to dispose of their dead. Therefore, these discoveries, made so quickly and in such high concentrations, did not lead to any arrests, and instead only acted to cement Murder Swamp's creepy reputation.

New Castle's swamp did not receive much attention outside the city until June 1936, when a second rash of bodies was discovered in abandoned boxcars located near the marsh. County police began their investigation promptly, but had no sooner started to dig around when news out of Ohio made them think it might be smart to bring in some out-of-state investigators for a second look.

Beginning in the fall of 1935, Cleveland had experienced an onslaught of unsolved, violent crimes that bore the mark of a serial killer. The first victim was found in September by two boys who were playing on Jackass Hill, a ratty area of Cleveland's Kingsbury Run. Located along the east side of the city, Kingsbury Run resembled Murder Swamp in a number of ways. Both were overgrown plots of land, filled with weeds, trash, and itinerants who didn't have the wherewithal to seek more hospitable shelter. Like New Castle's swamp, Kingsbury Run was abutted by a river (the Cuyahoga), and very sparsely populated; in fact, most all of those who could be found at the Run were homeless themselves.

The first body found in Cleveland—a white male wearing only black socks—was missing both his head and his genitals. A police search of the area prompted the discovery of a second body. This male victim, who appeared markedly older than the first, had also been decapitated and was without his genitals. Both bodies were positioned on their backs, with their arms placed neatly against their torsos and their legs spread wide open. The heads and genitals of both men were found buried in the area. Fingerprints taken from the younger victim identified him as Edward Andrassy, a twenty-eight-year-old known in the area as a sometimes-violent drunk.

According to Troy Taylor, who writes the blog prairieghosts .com, the forensic examination of the bodies revealed "puzzling evidence. The body of the older man turned out to be badly decomposed and the skin discolored from some sort of solution that the pathologists believed had been used to try and preserve it. The man had been dead for about two weeks and yet someone had [not immediately disposed of the body], only dumping it when it had become too decayed to keep any longer." The examination also determined that victim "[Edward] Andrassy had actually died from the decapitation." In other words, when his feet and hands were bound by ropes, he was perfectly alert, and able to "struggle violently" up until his head was removed. The immediate determination made by the Cleveland Police Department was that the city was dealing with a murderer who was both strong enough to subdue a grown man and knowledgeable enough about medicine to make moves to preserve victims' bodies.

Thanks to the gruesome details surrounding the murders and the lack of any sort of crime scene (neither victim's body was bloody, and no blood was found in the area where either body was discovered), the press quickly jumped on the story, deeming the killer the "Mad Butcher of Kingsbury Run." Members of the Cleveland press were serious about sensationalizing the murders; meanwhile, local politicians offered hope that the killer would be caught, thanks to the 1935 appointment of Eliot Ness as the town's safety director. Ness had made himself famous due largely to his success shutting down the likes of Al Capone; now, in taking on this new serial killer, Ness was about to become more scrutinized than ever.

No new leads had been uncovered in the case of the Mad Butcher when, during January 1936, the torso of a female body—missing all of its limbs except its right arm—was discovered within a few miles of where the Cuyahoga River traces Kingsbury Run. A fingerprint search revealed that the victim was a forty-one-year-old prostitute named Flo Polillo. Polillo's was the first female body located in Kingsbury Run. If her death was, indeed, the handiwork of Cleveland's Mad Butcher, the theory that the killer had targeted male victims—possibly as a form of targeted homosexual aggression—was blown apart. The appearance of Flo's body also brought to mind the torso of a Jane Doe who had been found near Lake Erie back in 1934. If they were to include this 1934 victim (nicknamed "victim zero" by the police) in with the Butcher's head count, authorities felt like they were back at square one, as the crimes did not appear to be held together by any discernible pattern.

Apparently taking the winter off—at least in Cleveland—the Butcher's work did not surface again until the summer of 1936, when two young boys discovered a severed head wrapped inside of a pair of pants lying beneath a Kingsbury Run bridge. When police later discovered the body—heavily tattooed—a quarter mile away, they noted that, unlike previous crime scenes, this one contained enough blood to suggest an on-site murder. Forensic analysis was able to determine that this man died from decapitation, although police couldn't find any weapon or equipment in the area that could have been used in such a crime. A few weeks after, during July, a fifth headless Butcher victim was discovered in a ravine. This male's body was badly decomposed, indicating he had been killed much earlier than the tattooed victim.

Before summer's end, another male victim was found in Kingsbury Run. Like the men before him, this victim was missing both his head and his genitals. In a new twist, the Butcher had also cut this man cleanly in two. A hat found in the area was a celebrated clue, as a neighborhood woman was able to identify it as the hat she had donated to a homeless man. This discovery led police to believe that their murderer was in the habit of preying on squatters living in Kingsbury's "hobo camps." The trouble

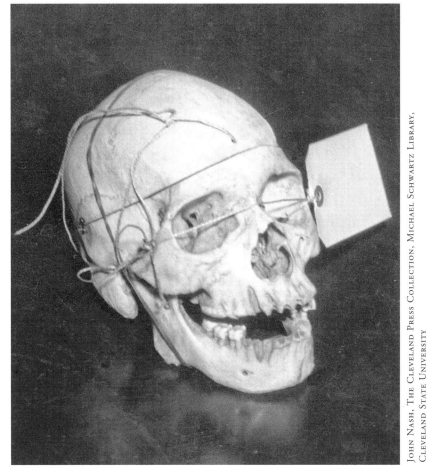

Skull of Torso Murder victim.

JOHN NASH, THE CLEVELAND PRESS COLLECTION, MICHAEL SCHWARTZ LIBRARY, CLEVELAND STATE UNIVERSITY

with this pool of victims was that they were incredibly transient and generally unmotivated to cooperate with police.

By the end of summer, it had become obvious that the Butcher, now earning a second nickname of the Torso Killer, was not interested in stopping the ongoing murder spree. In response, Eliot Ness asked John Flynn, his assistant safety director, and one of his top detectives, Peter Merlyo, to determine whether similar crimes had happened outside of Cleveland. When word came in from county police up near New Castle, Pennsylvania, it felt like the team was given an investigative windfall.

On September 16, 1936, Flynn and a few of his detectives traveled ninety miles southeast to New Castle, to meet with Police Chief Ralph Criswell, who offered his services as both a historian and a tour guide. First, Criswell told the Ohioans about Murder Swamp's initial string of dead bodies, which, back in 1925, the county police had chalked up to the site's reputation as a mob and gang dumping ground. But the summer of 1936 had brought on a new set of victims, ones that looked like they might not be gang victims, given what had been going on in Cleveland.

At the very end of June, Oscar Wukovich, a man many locals considered to be the only resident of Murder Swamp, reported that he'd seen a cast of hawks circling over a group of abandoned boxcars. The birds caught Wukovich's attention, especially because he knew that, for the past five years, inspectors from the Pittsburgh & Lake Erie Railroad Company had regularly checked the train cars (in fact, they had been out to the site on June 10). Wukovich's alarm prompted two company inspectors to report to the swamp where, on July 1, they found evidence of a crime. Inside one of the twenty-three abandoned boxcars was the naked, headless body of a male. The victim, positioned face down, was lying on top of newspapers. Chief Criswell was quick to tell the visiting members of the Cleveland PD that under this body were pages from an issue of Cleveland's daily newspaper, the *Plain Dealer*. The head, Criswell explained, had yet to be found.

John Flynn returned to Cleveland only half-convinced that the Murder Swamp victim was the work of the Kingsbury Run Butcher. True, it would have been easy for the Butcher to travel between the two locations by freight, but it was just as likely that the Pennsylvania crime was the work of a copycat killer. Both Flynn and his boss knew that as the scrutiny surrounding the department's handling of the case grew, they needed to be increasingly more cautious about what information they shared with the press. So, during the early fall of 1936, the official party line was that "there was nothing definite to link the New Castle slaying to the Torso murders."

The saga that would continue in Cleveland surrounding the Kingsbury Run Butcher was overwrought with a suspense that was never fully quelled. The next victim was found in February 1937, when a torso belonging to an unidentified female was discovered near Lake Erie. Soon after, another female body was unearthed. Identified by her teeth as Mrs.

Rose Wallace, her body was so badly decomposed that authorities determined that she might have actually been killed the year prior. The Butcher's ninth victim was another male who had been decapitated and mutilated. Following this, pieces of a woman's body were found inside of two burlap bags. Although the Torso Murderer was giving the coroner more and more flesh to inspect, police remained stymied about both the killer's identity and motive. In fact, because the Butcher's work was so meticulous, many believed that the primary key to catching the villain was to identify the location (often imagined as a laboratory) where many of the victims had been beheaded and their bodies drained of blood.

When, during the close of 1937, nobody stumbled upon any bodies, and no limbs washed ashore alongside Lake Erie or the Cuyahoga, Clevelanders began to wonder if the Butcher had gone silent. Then, during August 1938, the dismembered body of a woman was found in Kingsbury Run; when police were searching for evidence, they discovered the body of yet another (male) victim. As Troy Taylor reports, "Finally certain that the Butcher was selecting . . . victims from the homeless and down and out's of Kingsbury Run, Ness took a drastic step. Two days after the police found the last two bodies, officers raided the shantytown that was located in the ravine. They arrested hundreds of vagrants and burned down the shelters, shacks, and shanties. Whether it was a coincidence or a brilliant move on the part of Eliot Ness, the murders stopped."

There are many theories that speculate about why the Cleveland murders stopped. Some believe that Eliot Ness knew who the Mad Butcher was but lacked sufficient evidence to prosecute him. Those who subscribe to this theory have identified the murderer as Dr. Frank Sweeney. There were a number of reasons why Ness and Lieutenant David L. Cowles, superintendent of the ballistic bureau, believed Sweeney to be the Butcher: He was raised near Kingsbury Run; he was a medical doctor who had also received field training as a member of the Army Medical Corps during World War I; he was strong enough to have (alone) carried any one of the Butcher's victims; he was reportedly bisexual, possibly linking him to the removal of many of the male victim's genitalia; and he was a known alcoholic whose mood swings were reportedly fierce. Significantly, Sweeney was known to have checked himself into Sandusky, Ohio's Soldiers and Sailors Veteran's Home during the discovery of some of the Butcher's bodies. Because his stays there were voluntary, he was able to come and go as he pleased, leaving police to suspect that his hospital stays were evidence of a well-crafted alibi.

The trail leading to Sweeney does seem damning, and perhaps it would have been officially pursued had the doctor not been the first cousin of Congressman Martin L. Sweeney. As described by journalist Marilyn Bardsley, the Congressman was "a very colorful and controversial political powerhouse in the local Democratic Party" who was not shy about his disdain for Eliot Ness. So, although police questioned him, Dr. Sweeney was never arrested for the crime. Instead, in August 1939, a man named Frank Dolezal confessed to the murder of Flo Polillo (the Butcher's third victim). Although it is likely that Dolezal would have been tried for many of the Butcher's murders, he hung himself in a Cleveland prison before the matter could be addressed in court. Many believed that Dolezal was a fall guy, handpicked by police to placate the worried public.

As is easy to imagine, without any clear resolution conspiracy theories surrounding the Torso Murderer did not die out, even when the victims stopped surfacing. Cleveland Detective Peter Merlyo was so devoted to the case that he worked it even after his retirement from the department. Crime buffs from as far away as California had also become invested, as many of them saw links between the Butcher's handiwork and the manner in which Elizabeth Short (later renamed the "Black Dahlia" by the Hollywood press) was gruesomely sliced in half, drained of blood, and left to be found in a public park.

While Cleveland and those interested parties nationwide struggled to reconcile the work of the Mad Butcher, New Castle had continued on, business as usual. That is, until October 1939, when the headless body of a man was discovered in Murder Swamp. As if not to slip into obscurity, the victim—whose head was later discovered in an abandoned boxcar—was positioned next to newspapers published one-month earlier in Youngstown, Ohio, a town located twenty miles from New Castle, and just under seventy-five miles from Cleveland. The following year, three bodies were found inside of three boxcars. As author Thomas White details, "Inside each of the cars were the dismembered corpses of two unidentified men and one woman. They had been dead for several months. One of the victims had the word 'Nazi' with an inverted *z* carved into his chest. After investigating, Merlyo discovered that the cars had been sent from Youngstown." Another headless corpse was found in Pittsburgh in 1939. In 1941, two legs were found floating along the Ohio River. The following year saw the discovery of yet another decapitated corpse in the Monongahela River. And in 1950 Cleveland was host to one last beheaded torso, identified as Robert Robertson, who was discovered near Lake Erie during the middle of the summer.

The killer (or killers) who dismembered both Pennsylvanians and Ohioans during the mid-1900s will certainly be remembered for both a meticulous style and an ability to disappear into the overgrown brush of abandoned lands. While there is no concrete evidence to determine whether the Butcher started a mad killing spree using Murder Swamp as an early dumping ground before moving on to crimes in Kingsbury Run, many who live in and around New Castle believe the Torso Murderer was responsible for the intermittent spikes in their town's vicious deaths. There is no telling just how many limbs have yet to be discovered in the depths of Murder Swamp.

# CHAPTER 4

## *Unfathomable Conditions: Centralia's Burning Mine Fire*

Ignoring the lonely and brokenhearted, February 14, 1981, began normally enough. The sun was spilling generously over Centralia, a small town located just over one hundred miles northwest of Philadelphia. The neighborhood knew its own, as most all of its residents were second- or third-generation citizens. On this particular Saturday, the town was playing host to some outsiders: Congressman James Nelligan, Senator Edward Helfrick, and the acting director of the Office of Surface Mining, Andrew Bailey. The men had convened at Nelligan's behest, based upon the newly elected Congressman's hope that they could help Centralia begin to suffocate the mine fire that had been burning under the town since 1962.

Curious about who these men in suits were, and what their business in town was, Todd Domboski's mother sent her twelve-year-old son out on foot, angling to figure out what, exactly, was going on. En route he encountered a cousin who happened to be fixing a flat tire in their grandmother's backyard. As Todd consulted with Erik, the boys noticed a stream of smoke snaking out from the ground, not too far from where they were standing. In an investigative mindset, Todd approached the smoke, not knowing that he was, in the truest sense, playing with fire.

As the story was later told, within thirty seconds the ground had completely dropped out from beneath Todd. Like a mossy quicksand, the earth sucked his feet and crawled up his shins, inching towards his knees with alarming speed. By the time he heard himself calling out to Erik, he was already waist deep, sinking into the mud and drawing ever closer to the fire burning beneath his feet. Feeling helpless against gravity's ominous pull, Todd struggled against the soil, grasping for anything that would help slow his plummet. The smoke and steam were raging hot below his feet, stinking of sulfur. This was a disaster in the making.

It must have looked like a lost cause when Erik came to his cousin's rescue. Here Todd was, almost fully buried in the sinking earth, in foggy haze created by the boiling earth as it rose closer to the ground's surface. As journalist Joan Quigley recounts, "Erik sprinted over and dropped to his stomach. Peering into the hole, two feet wide and swirling with hot white vapors, he could barely discern the outlines of Todd's orange hat, about six feet down." Todd was doing his best to hold strong, with both his back and his feet braced against the sides of the hole. It was from this position that Todd and Erik were able to lock hands, using strength beyond themselves to extricate Todd from the dangerous well. And, to their shock, despite being muddy and quite shaken, not an inch of Todd's body was burned.

Todd Domboski was not asking for trouble, but it's impossible to reverse your fate when you're dealing with a fire that just won't quit. Centralia hadn't always been plagued by such hardship—in the late nineteenth century it was an idyllic coal town whose population registered just under 2,800. However, while the tiny town was initially celebrated for the anthracite coal that sits underneath its rolling hills, this blessing would soon turn into the town's biggest curse.

Anthracite coal is unique due to its high carbon content. As a substance, it is much harder and blacker than more common variants of coal. While physicists and geologists could smartly detail all of anthracite coal's characteristics, for the purposes of evaluating its presence in and around Centralia, three basic facts should be noted: Anthracite coal is rare in the United States (only scant quantities exist outside of Eastern Pennsylvania); it burns cleaner than other variants of coal and is therefore a more desirable source of power; and it sells for double or even triple the cost of more common bituminous types of coal.

The discovery of anthracite coal in Northeast Pennsylvania prompted miners and employees of the Locust Mountain Coal and Iron Company to settle in the area now known as Centralia. Founded in 1866 (and originally given the name Centerville), Centralia grew according to the needs of its residents, peaking in the late nineteenth century with a population just under three thousand.

The men and boys who worked in the fourteen mines that were created in the area had incredibly difficult jobs. Author Michael Hannon estimated that, between "the years 1870–1901, the number of those killed in the anthracite industry was 10,318, while the number of those nonfatally injured during the same period was 27,311." The dangerous conditions certainly contributed to the anthracite coal strike of 1902, which lasted 163 days and concluded only after federal intervention (this labor struggle is addressed at a greater length in Chapter Seven). While miners were breathing a collective sigh of relief after negotiations yielded shorter working days and somewhat better safety regulations, hindsight tells us that Centralia should actually have begun bracing for the bad times to follow.

The stock market crash of 1929 resulted in the demise of Lehigh Valley Coal Company, thereby destroying one of Centralia's largest employers at the time. As a result, many out-of-work miners accepted short-term work, strip-mining for coal companies. The work was labor intensive even though these strip-mining operations were temporary jobs. As author Joan Quigley describes, the strip miners "deployed steam shovels into coal seams at the easy-to-reach surface. Where mountains had once stood, laced with pines, birch trees, and mountain laurel, the strip miners left behind piles of black waste, often towering several stories high, and hollowed-out basins, some as long as football fields." Centralia's serene, small-town feel was quickly being replaced by evidence of how everyone was scraping just to get by.

While the strip miners were devastating what was left of Centralia's pastoral countryside, the earth below the town was beginning to resemble a complicated ant farm, laying the groundwork for the fire that would eventually ravage the area. Kevin Krajick, a journalist for *Smithsonian Magazine,* writes, "In the 19th and early 20th centuries, miners reached the anthracite deposits through mazes of tunnels, shafts and gangways. If a fire got started in them, miners were usually able to extinguish it before it spread. Then oil and gas replaced anthracite as premier home heating fuels. By the 1950s, most Pennsylvania anthracite mines had been abandoned. Entrances caved in; tunnels began to fill with rubble. Later, strip miners with modern equipment came at the coal from the surface, but they could never reach it all. The result was a landscape of stony debris on top of leftover underground coal laced by interconnected airways—a perfect setting for a coal fire."

The exact origin of Centralia's biggest (and still burning) mine fire is the cause of some dispute. Most agree that it began in the entrance of a mine, near Odd Fellows Cemetery, when piles of garbage were lit on fire. Most Centralians also acknowledge that, at the time, the site was being used as a town dump, brimming with mounds of flammable materials, ranging from soiled paper to discarded bed frames. The consensus is that the fire in question was first ignited on May 27, 1962. What is up for debate, however, is specifically who started the fire, and under what circumstances.

Some believe that locals, in the habit of burning their own trash, had started the blaze as a consequence of routine. Others believe that it was the local sanitation workers who set the landfill on fire. In fact, at least one historical source names Curly Stasulevich, a "commercial hauler," as having started the blaze when he dumped hot ashes onto the communal trash heap. Still others contend that the fire was purposefully set into motion by government officials, at the request of trustees from the nearby cemetery, who wanted the dump eradicated of its vermin and foul odors before the Memorial Day holiday.

No matter whose coals or match lit the blaze, no one felt an immediate sense of concern or urgency when they saw the dump on fire. Not only were garbage fires commonplace, they were sanctioned. During the first few months of 1962, the site had passed a Commonwealth inspection, and was certified as a safe space to house Centralia's new landfill. The permit was issued after holes created by previous mining attempts were filled with "incombustible materials." What was not discovered during said inspection is the fifteen-foot hole that happened to catch fire during the May blaze. This undetected chute, whose cavern remained unplugged, formed the groundwork for the disaster that would slowly demolish the entire town.

The folks in Centralia were from good, tough, Pennsylvania stock and were therefore, by all accounts, unfazed by the 1962 fire. As *Smithsonian* journalist Kevin Krajick detailed, that May they watched as local volunteer firefighters attempted to "flush" the mine's holes with a mixture of "wet sand, gravel, slurries of cement and fly ash to cut off oxygen." And, when the flames still burned, they stood by when small trenches were dug in unsuccessful efforts to head off the growing fire. In truth, most residents admittedly didn't even think much about the closing of nearby mines due to concerns about high underground carbon monoxide levels. Really, from all available accounts, life in Centralia after the 1962 fire moved forward with only the slightest of changes.

Some residents now talk about the initial ramifications of the burning fire with a bit of humor, telling how their vegetable gardens flourished well beyond summer months, and how fewer driveways needed to be plowed during the winter thanks to the heat radiating from below. Sure, the sight of officials from the Department of Environmental Resources was more common as a result of the landfill fire. And, while some suspected that the holes these men drilled to monitor the fire's expanse and temperature might have actually contributed to the strength of the blaze, during those early years no one thought to interrupt official business.

Hindsight tells us that if attempts to suffocate the fire had been made during the months and even the years following May 1962, stifling the fire would have been a feasible operation. But no such moves were made, even though it wasn't like the town was without ideas. In August 1962, a local strip miner named Alonzo Sanchez offered to dig trenches to isolate the fire when it was still in its infancy. But Sanchez's proposal was rejected under the auspices that the state was going to assume responsibility for extinguishing the fire. According to author David DeKok, Sanchez's additional proposition to "dig a pit three-quarters of a mile long and deep as a forty-five-story building, would have cost $660 million, more than the value of the property of the town," so it, too, was ignored. Therefore, without the intervention and/or financial assistance from government officials outside of Centralia, the town was left to muddle through, unprepared for its future.

The first real sign of concern came during May 1969, when the fire—now ravaging for seven straight years—forced three Centralia families out of their homes. Oddly, the town had (finally) started digging trenches earlier that month, but their progress was too slow to make any real progress. As Centralian Tony Gaughan would later remark, "If the trench had been dug in three shifts per day instead of one, and if they had worked through the Labor Day holiday, the fire would have been contained [in 1969]." But, as with most preventative measures, because no immediate danger was noted, no immediate assistance was provided.

The mandated exodus of three families was certainly tangible in a small, close-knit community like Centralia, but it was nothing compared to the national spotlight the town earned after the earth tried to swallow up Tom Domboski. All of a sudden, anyone who had been paying attention had plenty of evidence of the horrors awaiting the residents of Centralia. While Todd Domboski's story is fixed on Valentine's Day, 1981, John Coddington's day hit just one month later, on March 19. Coddington the former mayor of Centralia, was well known in the community. Having worked in the mines directly following high school, John saved up enough money to open his own gas station, which he ran while he and his wife, Isabelle, raised their son Joe. His years underground had given John a case of black lung, resulting in a shortness of breath that was common among those men who had cashed steady paychecks from big coal companies.

John and his family lived in an apartment located above his gas station on South Locust Avenue (just across the street from Todd Dombroski's grandmother's house). Thanks to their proximity to the fire, the Coddington's were among the Centralia residents whose homes had been outfitted with carbon monoxide monitors. For at least fifteen years, the machines had continuously printed receipts reflecting gas levels. The Coddingtons were used to it; indeed, most residents thought the electronic hum of the monitor was much less disruptive than the regular visits from state gas inspectors.

On March 19, the Coddingtons had gone out to dinner, returning home before the outside temperature dropped to about fifteen degrees. Notably, that evening the humidity was high, near 85 percent, which was dangerous in Centralia, as the heavy air held the fire's noxious gases close to the ground. John

Coddington had fallen asleep early by the television before his son encouraged him to just call it a night. Shortly before ten o'clock, Isabelle and Joe heard a thud coming from the bedroom; John had fallen from the bed and was gasping for air. Convinced he had suffered a heart attack, Isabelle Coddington called the ambulance and also some neighbors, who reported to the house without delay.

Upon the arrival of friends and medical personnel, someone had the wherewithal to check the oxygen level in the Coddington's house: It was at 18 percent, which should have triggered their monitor's alarm system (the system rang whenever levels dipped below 19.5). This information helped the doctor determine that, even though Coddington was exhibiting strokelike symptoms, he was actually suffering from oxygen deprivation. While the course of the evening's events certainly gave the Coddingtons a scare, his falling out of bed had turned him into the canary in the coal mine. As state inspector Edward Narcavage told Isabelle and Joe later that night, "You're lucky John fell off the bed. If he hadn't, and you'd just gone to bed, I don't think any of you would have woken up again."

As John Coddington proved, in Centralia it had become dangerous just go to sleep in your home, thanks to the insidious levels of carbon monoxide that crept into basements and up to bedrooms. But, it was arguably just as perilous to try to escape Centralia, as, Route 61—the town's main traffic artery—had sunk eight feet since it was paved, causing the asphalt to buckle as milky steam rose from the dramatic fissures. Repairs in the early 1980s did little to prevent longstanding damage to the road, which was ultimately shut down to vehicular traffic in 1994.

The fight as to what to do with Centralia and its residents dragged out over too many years. As congressmen and city council members tried to join forces, their voices were ignored by those in Harrisburg and, worse yet, by those in Washington. For every two Centralians who wanted the government to offer to buy their home, there were residents who couldn't imagine that there was a life worth living outside of their small town. Conspiracy theories emerged when, in 1983, a buyout began to seem probable, prompting folks to start wondering how much money the

GAIL HUGHES

The old Route 61 in Centralia, Pennsylvania, August 2011.

government could make mining the remaining anthracite coal once the neighborhood situated on top of it was demolished.

In 1983, after Centralians voted 345 to 200 in favor of relocation, Congress approved a bill that gave the town $42 million to assist in moving families out of danger. A group representing the Centralia Homeowners Association made the trip to Washington, DC, thankful to finally be able to celebrate a much overdue victory.

Not all of the town's residents moved out of harm's way, however. Even after the town's buildings were condemned in 1992, a handful of folks remain, apparently content to have the town to themselves. In 2008 there were an estimated eleven properties still being maintained, while steady throngs of tourists come to the town regularly, hoping to see evidence of the legendary and destructive fire.

# CHAPTER 5

## Unfathomable Conditions: Philadelphia's Teleportation Experiment

As he'd later tell it, the whole thing left him completely flummoxed. Carlos Allende said all he could do was stare at the Philadelphia harbor, dumbfounded. One second he was looking at a 1,240-ton destroyer, and before he could even gasp, it was nowhere in sight. The USS *Eldridge,* first laid down into the water in February 1943, had completely disappeared. It would get even worse. When the ship reappeared, a good many of the men on board were "molecularly attached" to its steel. Legs were adjoined with bulkheads, and hands were buried in ship walls. The screaming Allende must have heard—the nightmares that must have followed!

What would later become known as the Philadelphia Experiment occurred during the fall of 1943. Before a small crowd of onlookers, a Navy destroyer reportedly vanished from the Philadelphia Naval Yard, appeared in Norfolk, Virginia, and then returned to Philly holding a crew that was rattled or, worse yet, mutilated. Some contend that the ship's activity was not accidental. Instead, they believe that it was the direct result of testing designed by the Navy to determine whether teleportation was a feasible option to incorporate into World War II battle.

To fully understand the tale of the USS *Eldridge,* we must start with a heralded twentieth-century scientific figure: Albert Einstein. According to the US Department of the Navy, for two years during WWII, Dr. Einstein was a confirmed "part-time consultant with the Navy's Bureau of Ordnance, undertaking theoretical research on explosives and explosions." While there is no evidence to suggest that Einstein handled anything besides research to create better weapons, there are those who believe that the master of the unified field theory spent part of 1943 helping the Navy test whether they could teleport a ship from one place to another. After all, there may be no better weaponry than invisibility coupled with the capacity to reappear out of thin air.

The two men best known for having purported firsthand knowledge of the USS *Eldridge's* brief disappearance are Carlos Miguel Allende, identified by his seaman's number 7416175, and Alfred Bielek, a man who claimed to have unearthed memories of having served as a Navy scientist during the Philadelphia Experiment. Allende gained national attention in 1955, while Bielek reportedly regained his full memory in 1989.

Carlos Miguel Allende was born Carl Meredith Allen in Springfield, Pennsylvania, in 1925. According to his brothers, even as a young student, Carl was in the habit of annotating his books, filling the pages with questions, stray markings, and commentary that seemed to make complete sense only to him. According to family members, after finishing a book, he was apt to mail it to "someone who might take interest," whether that be a neighbor or a stranger. As his brother, David Allen, told the documentarians of A&E's *History's Mysteries* series in 2008, "He was very intelligent, and, but, not really smart if you know what I mean."

According to his seaman's record, by the time the Navy snapped his photograph for his identification card, Carl M. Allen had begun to call himself Carlos Miguel Allende. He then began to use this name, and, at times, his seaman's number, when signing the various letters and books he sent around the country in an effort to educate others with the inner workings of his mind. No one seems to know just how expansive his address book was. Although we don't know his intentions, it has been documented that, in 1955, Allende sent a book to the Office of Naval Research. Allende's package was addressed to (a nonexistent) Admiral N. Furth, sent from Seminole, Texas, and featured the message "HAPPY EASTER" on the back of its manila envelope.

It is impossible to estimate whether Allende had a sinister plan when he sent his annotated copy of Morris K. Jessup's *The Case of the UFO* to the Office of Naval Research. But, his package was certainly well timed. In the 1950s, the Navy established Project Blue Book, designed to investigate the existence of unidentified flying objects (UFOs) as well as to ascertain whether reports of UFOs posed a security threat to the nation. Because there was no Admiral Furth on site, Allende's mail wound up on the desks of Lieutenant Commander George Hoover and Captain Sidney Sherby; fortuitously, Hoover believed in UFOs, and Sherby had recently grown suspicious of how the Navy's investigations into the paranormal seemed to operate like a "sink," where official determinations were never announced or publicized.

Upon opening the package, the men discovered that they had just been gifted a book whose pages were littered with messages written enthusiastically in all caps and three different colors of ink. Famously, one of Allende's margin notes reads: "US NAVY'S FORCEFIELD EXPERIMENTS OCTOBER PRODUCED INVISIBILITY OF SHIP + CREW FEARSOME RESULTS SO TERRIFYING AS TO, FORTUNATELY, HALT FURTHER RESEARCH."

While perhaps not fully alarmed, Lt. Cdr. Hoover and Capt. Sherby felt the package warranted further investigation. Together, the men reached out to Jessup, a scientist and writer who had spent his professional career trying to legitimize the existence of UFOs. Upon meeting with the Navy researchers, Jessup admitted that he recognized sections of the marginalia, as he himself had received tricolored notes from an individual with the same penmanship. With Jessup's approval, Capt. Sherby ordered a few hundred copies of *UFO* printed to include Allende's notes. This version of the book became known as the *UFO* Varo edition.

When word got out that researchers from the Office of Naval Research had received a pro-UFO book full of mysterious (and possibly insightful) scrawl, rumors began to circulate that an alien had sent the book to the government. And, when folks began to clamor for their own Varo edition and no copies were made available to the public, a frenzy started to form. There is arguably no better way to fuel a simmering conspiracy theory than by learning that a government entity is withholding information from curious citizens. All of a sudden, people began to really believe that government officials knew how to teleport objects. While what happened in Philadelphia was an experiment, no one knew what might come next.

The creation and subsequent suppression of the Varo edition of M. K. Jessup's book marks the moment when the legend of the Philadelphia Experiment was officially born. The events that followed cemented Jessup's place in the fabric of continuing speculation about supposed UFO secrets and intrigue. It is said that, following his meeting with Naval Research officers, Jessup began conducting his own investigation into the legitimacy of Carlos Allende's annotated notes. By April 1959, Jessup is reported to have discovered something in Allende's notes that was powerful enough that he immediately felt the need to share it with his friend and colleague, Dr. J. Manson Valentine. The discovery was so big that Jessup insisted that they meet in person to discuss it. However, the day before the two were to meet, Jessup was found in Coral Gables, Florida, dead of an apparent suicide by carbon monoxide poisoning. While some close to Jessup speculated that he was depressed following a recent divorce and the lack of respect his UFO literature had garnered, those who were most invested in his paranormal research detected a cover-up.

During the next decade, Carlos Miguel Allende continued sending letters here and there and remained in the practice of mailing books to random individuals. Those close to Allende would later talk about his being miffed that he reaped no financial benefits when others would sell his letters and scribbles. It wasn't just civilians who were making money off of his correspondence; magazines, too, were publishing his letters to increase subscription numbers and sales. Seemingly fed up with being the only one who wasn't benefiting from his firsthand account of the 1943 Naval Yard experiment, in 1969 Carlos Allende identified himself as the "alien" responsible for the Varo edition text, along with countless other missives. The announcement was made after Allende walked into the Aerial Phenomena Research Organization's headquarters, in Tucson, Arizona, claiming that everything he had recorded about the Philadelphia Experiment was the "wildest pack of lies [he] ever wrote."

Though news of Allende's confession was published, it seemed to do very little damage to the legacy his letters had created. In truth, the lore that Allende had spun just would not die. In 1979, its notoriety received a boost when Charles Berlitz (author of the wildly popular book *The Bermuda Triangle*) teamed up with William L. Moore to write *Philadelphia Experiment: Project*

*Invisibility.* It was no small coincidence that, after the book started selling out of stores, Carlos Allende reemerged on the scene, seemingly oblivious to his own 1969 confession to being a fraud.

The public, or at least the portion of the public most intrigued by reports of paranormal activity, were happy to welcome Allende back. It could be argued that his stories became even more enthralling following the publication of *Project Invisibility,* as Allende—no longer just a name—was now able to speak freely and publically about his 1943 role of eyewitness.

At this time, one new story of a barroom brawl emerged, adding to the story of the Philadelphia Experiment. According to Allende, some members of the skeleton crew aboard the USS *Eldridge* were not physically injured as a result of the teleportation. Despite this, the men were shaky from the ordeal, and decided to calm their nerves at a nearby watering hole. As one drink led to another, the sailors found themselves fighting with a few fellow patrons. According to Allende, there were eyewitnesses who swore that, during the fight, the sailors had disappeared in and out of sight, throwing punches one minute and fading from view the next. The identity of these seamen—so obviously affected by teleportation—was withheld from their families, who instead were told by the Navy that the sailors were missing in action.

In 1994, a reporter from *THE NEWS* of Colorado Centennial Country wrote a story containing Allende's alleged "death bed statement," which revealed his dying belief that he not only was witness to the Philadelphia Experiment, but that he had also

US Department of State—O'Donnell. National Archives/Naval History and Heritage Command

USS *Eldridge* (DE-173) and USS *Garfield Thomas* (DE-193), January 1951.

interfaced with Einstein throughout and following the Experiment. "Right now," he told reporter Jim Frazier, "there are only four men in the United States who understand Unified Field Theory. I am one of them—but I am not a scientist. My knowledge is from experience and from time with Einstein. He taught me what he could and made me understand."

Miraculously, Carl Allen's death did not put an end to incoming eyewitness accounts of the Philadelphia Experiment. While Allende's vantage point of the USS *Eldridge* was quite close—he was, after all, reportedly in the same harbor as the USS *Eldridge*—Alfred Bielek became the preeminent witness to the Experiment when, in 1989, he announced that he was actually on the *Eldridge* when it teleported out of Pennsylvania.

Bielek, who passed away in October 2011, wrote and spoke extensively about his involvement in the Philadelphia Experiment. It should be noted that, while Bielek said that his half-brother, Duncan Cameron, was also a scientist who participated in the experiment, it seems that Duncan did not share his brother's penchant for discussing the events that took place aboard the USS *Eldridge*. It should also be noted that neither Bielek's nor Cameron's names appear on Naval paperwork, and original crew members of the ship have no recollection of their presence on the destroyer. (In fact, these crew members universally swear that the ship never even touched the waters of a Philadelphia harbor.)

As a self-appointed expert, Al Bielek contended that the Philadelphia Experiment occurred over three days: July 22, August 12, and a day in late October of 1943. Bielek, whose rank in the military remains unknown, is colorful when describing how it felt to be on the *Eldridge* during the first official teleportation test. As Bielek told attendees at the January 13, 1990, MUFON Conference (see www.mufon.com to learn more about MUFON), of the twenty-two crew members, he was responsible for activating teleportation by turning on the generators (designed, in part, by Nikola Tesla and Dr. John von Neumann). Bielek said that he did not feel anything remarkable during the fifteen to twenty minutes that the generators were running, even though the ship had apparently vanished from the harbor during this time. But, upon returning to port, he and his crew members discovered "there was a serious problem."

Bielek regaled attendees at the MUFON Conference with his stories of the after-effects of teleportation. (It should be noted that the acronym MUFON, formerly representing Midwest UFO Network, now stands for Mutual UFO Network, thus reflecting the group's current worldwide base.) According to Bielek, those seamen who were above deck were "totally disoriented, nauseous, throwing up" and acting obviously delirious. The Navy's reported response was to blame the state of affairs on a "personnel issue," and so they moved to quickly assemble a new crew. According to Bielek, despite the pleas of Dr. Von Neumann, who wanted to study how and why the teleportation had sent so many of the seamen into hysterics, Naval officials insisted that things move along rapidly. Without explanation, the crew was given a "drop-date" of August 12, 1943, just a few weeks from their initial teleportation run.

If Bielek's account of the July run sounds concerning, the details he shared with the MUFON attendees concerning the August test sits somewhere between bewildering and gruesome. According to his account, after he flipped the switch to activate the ship's generator, the USS *Eldridge* disappeared for four hours, relocating forty years in the future. Bielek contended that, upon leaving the ship, he and his brother were greeted by a future version of Dr. Von Neumann. The scientist explained to the Bielek brothers that they were visiting the Phoenix Project at Montauk, Long Island. After apprising his old shipmates of what life was like in 1983, Dr. Von Neumann reportedly instructed, "Gentlemen you have to go back and shut off the equipment on the *Eldridge;* this has already occurred according to our records, but it hasn't actually happened in reality." As Bielek would attest, the forty-year link between the Philadelphia Experiment and the Phoenix Project "created a hole in hyperspace." If the crew of the *Eldridge* failed to return safely to Philadelphia, a portion of reality itself would disappear. Al said that, at Von Neumann's request, he boarded the *Eldridge* and returned to Philadelphia, while his brother "followed orders" and "wound up in '83." The ship then returned to Philadelphia.

Once back in safe harbor, Navy scientists boarded the ship to find not only broken gear, but a broken crew. Some of the crew had literally fused with the ship, where portions of their bodies were "embedded in the steel decks" or in the ship's bulkheads. Bielek described the total chaos of the situation: "People running around totally bananas, and really insane, out of it. People who were appearing and disappearing." Bielek offered that he even saw shipmen who were burned beyond recognition. Thankfully, because Bielek had been below deck during both phases of the teleportation, he was spared such disorientation and disfiguration.

According to Al Bielek, the final teleportation occurred on a night in late October, around ten o'clock, when the USS *Eldridge* left Philadelphia and appeared three hundred miles away in Norfolk, Virginia, for roughly ten to fifteen minutes. Strangely, Bielek downplayed the last time that the *Eldridge* teleported, acknowledging that there is already an "apocrypha of stories" concerning this final teleportation. Bielek was right: The literature, film, and now web coverage of the supposed experiment is plentiful, even as the confirmed crew of the USS *Eldridge* and people old enough to remember Project Blue Book have begun to pass away.

The mystery promised by the Philadelphia Experiment is great: Invisibility could help us to accomplish (and destroy) so much, while the ability to teleport from one place to the next would shatter the very way that we live our lives. But, as H. Jeffrey Kimble, a Professor of Physics at Caltech, posits, "The notion that one could teleport a material system with any sense of size is just beyond technical capabilities for any foreseeable future."

While scientific logic undermines the assertion that, in 1943, the American Navy had the technology to make a 1,240-ton destroyer optically invisible in order to teleport it, available evidence does suggest that, during World War II, the Navy was working on rendering certain ships invisible to magnetic mines. As writer and historian Robert Goerman explained, "degaussing" is accomplished by "running wires along the hull of a ship." Crew members are asked to take off their watches and remove any clocks from the ship, as the degaussing process can alter the magnetic fields of timekeeping equipment. The end result of degaussing is that the ship will not be vulnerable to mine attack. While degaussing is a far cry from teleportation, some historians have questioned whether an overheard discussion of sailors talking about invisibility to magnetic mines was misconstrued, ultimately generating the much more exciting theory of total invisibility.

Between the stories given to us by both Carlos Allende and Alfred Bielek, we are let into a world that is much more fascinating than our own, where Einstein will give personalized lessons in unified field theory, and men can teleport forty years into the future and return unscathed. In the end, thanks to Allende and Bielek, we are left with a very real sense of how the lore of the Philadelphia Experiment began, in addition to understanding how it became inserted into the pantheon of celebrated conspiracy theories.

# CHAPTER 6

## *Unfathomable Conditions: Philadelphia's Eastern State Penitentiary*

You are a prisoner. It's 1829, and you are sentenced to Philadelphia's newly built Eastern State Penitentiary. You have indoor plumbing and central heating. You have your own room, complete with a small skylight, as well as your own private yard. You are given three square meals per day. If you do not have a trade, you are taught how to become an adept cobbler, weaver, or woodworker. You are able to give half of your salary to your family. You can read for endless hours. You may have personalized meetings with a spiritual leader of your choosing as frequently as you'd like. You can make any complaints you have against guards to the facility overseers and, if the overseers are at fault, you can lodge your concern with the warden, whom you see twice per month. You are going to begin living in what author Susan Hutchison Tassin deemed to be "the most expensive American structure ever built [at the time], costing $772,600." But, you have to make a few concessions . . .

Indoor plumbing is a new phenomenon, so your room smells musty, like sewage. You are not able to leave your room, except during the two half-hour periods each day that you are allowed to access your outdoor space, much like a boarded dog that has its own special run at the kennel. The food the guards give to you is slipped into your cell by a "feeding hole," which is a small space that connects your room to the interior of the prison. The only true door in your cell faces the courtyard, and it is quite drafty in the wintertime. Unless you work in the kitchen, you labor without leaving your cell. You are mandated to hand over half of your earnings to the county where you were sentenced. The one book you are given to read is the Bible. You only may see your family once every three months. But wait, it gets worse.

When you were first brought into Eastern State, you were given a wrap to wear that resembled a monk's robe. But, unlike the robe of the monk, which covers only the crown of the head, your robe draped from the top of your head down over your neck, masking your entire face. Your hood's eyeholes were small and prevented you from using your peripheral vision; your breath was hot as it sunk into the fabric held against your mouth. You were given a number, and as you've come to find out, your number quickly became your name.

That first night you were left alone, you thought about the advice you had been given, that all you had to do was get through the first day or two. Thinking back on this, you feel foolish, even naïve. You now know that it gets worse every night. While you can talk to the overseers and the warden every now and again, you don't ever see anyone else: You don't interact with other prisoners, there is no mess hall, and when you go outside, no one else on your row is outdoors at the same time as you. Although you can't figure out how, exactly, the guards sneak up to your cell from out of nowhere, they do quietly, wearing socks over their shoes to mute their steps. The silence of your everyday life is beyond deafening—it is unfathomable.

The concept that prompted the creation of Eastern State Penitentiary was first introduced in the late eighteenth century. According to author Susan Hutchison Tassin, in the late 1700s, "a Quaker group called the Philadelphia Society for Alleviating the Miseries of Public Prisons approached Benjamin Franklin with their belief that the current state of prisoners in America was deplorable. The Society's goal was to devise a new system for approaching incarceration: implementing a penitentiary." Specifically, the Society "wanted to build a prison that was designed to induce true regret in the criminal, causing the prisoner to reflect on his or her crime and do penance for it."

Originally called "Cherry Hill" because it was built on a cherry orchard, Eastern State Penitentiary (ESP) opened in 1829 with 250 prisoners. Architect John Haviland's design resembled that of a spider, with seven one-story cell blocks stretching out like limbs anchored to the facility's octagonal hub. As the prison population continued to grow, the cell blocks would increase both in number and in height; however the twelve-acre property itself was finite, surrounded by thirty-foot walls reminiscent of a medieval castle. Charles Williams, a Pennsylvanian sentenced to two years for stealing a horse, was the penitentiary's first prisoner. The room where Williams stayed for twenty-four months between 1829 and 1831 was actually more modern than the White House, where President Andrew Jackson had neither running water nor central heat.

With the cushion of a very large budget, Haviland sought not only to create a state-of-the-art space, but also a facility that offered convenience, ease of surveillance, economy, and good ventilation. Most would argue that Haviland's prison became famous because, unlike the more common congregate systems of incarceration (called the "Auburn System"), ESP was originally designed so that there were no common spaces for prisoners to assemble. It could be argued that part of the reason Haviland's bid was accepted by the state of Pennsylvania was not necessarily because it was particularly innovative, but because it was so clearly synchronized with philosophies of the Philadelphia Society for Alleviating the Miseries of Public Prisons. In an act written in 1790 concerning punishment and reformation, the Society outlined what would later serve as the foundation for ESP's operation and practice: "It may be assumed as a principle that the prospect of a long, solitary confinement, hard labour, and a very plain diet, would, to many minds, prove more terrible than even an execution, where this is the case, the operation of example would have its full effect, so far as it tended to deter others from commission of crime."

It was a phenomenon many wanted to see firsthand. The number of visitors who traveled to Eastern State was outrageously high—during the 1840s the prison welcomed roughly one hundred visitors daily—as many wanted to understand just how such a large complex could feasibly cater to each individual inmate. While some were wowed by Eastern State's separate or "Pennsylvania System," most felt it impossible to ignore how thoroughly, perhaps even unbearably, isolating life was at ESP.

The Quakers, historically known as a pacifist and pious group, seem to have believed that this kind of isolation would lead to great reflection, after which a prisoner would feel compelled to right himself. But, in practice, many believed that, "Eastern officials hoped that prohibiting all social intercourse among prisoners would literally strike terror in the hearts of inmates." When Charles Dickens visited the prison in 1842, he described ESP prisoners as being "buried alive; to be dug out in the slow sound of years; and in the meantime dead to everything but torturing anxieties and horrible despair." Prison reformer Frederick Wines also argued against the Pennsylvania System, asserting that, while solitude might drive a man mad, the Pennsylvania System's "program of silence" would lead men straight into rebellion.

Take, for example, the practice of giving prisoners monks' robes—one strong component of this isolating system. According

SONIA BERLIN

Eastern State Penitentiary, February 2012.

to author Francis X. Dolan, "The original, eyeless hoods" and later the hoods with small eye slits "ke[pt] the inmates in the dark about the layout of the prison," so as to thwart escape attempts. Additionally, early prison literature suggests that the anonymity of the hoods ensured that guards and prisoners would be unable to recognize one another after an inmate was released, thereby eliminating the possibility of undue stigma being given to a changed man. But, beyond these practical ramifications, the hoods also held heavy psychological effects. As Dolan posited, donning the hoods was "akin to a man being brought to the gallows." Charles Dickens, who was an outspoken opponent of the penitentiary's practices, deemed the prisoner hood a "dark shroud, an emblem of the curtain dropped between him and the living world."

Besides limiting prisoners' sightlines, ESP officials also restricted inmates' access to all forms of information. No news from the outside world was allowed into the penitentiary, which meant that prisoners were forbidden from receiving mail and reading the newspaper. Moreover, guards were prohibited from talking to prisoners and to one another. Prisoners who were caught talking—or tapping on walls or pipes in an effort to communicate with a neighbor—lost a meal or two. If the transgression was severe enough, blanket privileges could be taken away, or the prisoner might be subjected to a "shower bath," by being doused with cold water while wearing minimal clothing: Both of these punishments were obviously made worse by Philadelphia's often brutal winters. It is said that, because the silence was so uncomfortable, during ESP's early years, some guards got into the habit of bringing in alcohol to drink during their shifts, so as to ease the numbing boredom of the prison's environment and atmosphere. In fact, "at one point the guards were given a daily ration of liquor during the day in an attempt to prevent them from overindulging."

Immoderation was a true concern for prison officials, as such excess undermined the Quaker system of thoughtful repentance. According to author Timothy Gilfoyle, officials "acknowledged that the separate system stimulated certain undesirable sexual behaviors. By 1870, prison administrators recognized that with individual isolation, the inmate was 'still free to indulge in solitary vice,' in other words, masturbation. Eastern officials blamed masturbation for insanity and other problems."

Insanity—especially the incarceration of the insane—was the subject of great debate at the time. According to Susan Hutchison Tassin, "mental illness, not surprisingly, was a constant issue at Eastern State Penitentiary, although the management of the penitentiary downplayed its prevalence. The isolation, the sensory deprivation, the punishments, the uncomfortable living conditions, and the loss of many things that make one a human being drove many prisoners to madness."

At a meeting held in 1884, then prison warden Michael Cassidy was interrogated by an investigative legislative committee, who questioned him with regard to how Eastern State handled their population of mentally unbalanced inmates. Cassidy told the committee that of the fifty mentally unstable persons in the prison, only five had become so after admission. After offering this statistic, Cassidy acknowledged that the insane prisoners were "the source of a great deal of trouble." Although the committee seemed placated by his appearance at the hearing, the question of insanity at ESP was not an issue that disappeared quickly. In 1897, warden Cassidy was again made to answer to the committee. This time around, his response concerning his prison population was much more vague. First, he sought to impress upon the committee how difficult it is to determine whether an inmate is insane. Second, he offered the standard ESP strategy of taking unruly prisoners outside and "working" them for hours at a time. The syntax Cassidy used to describe his inmates is reminiscent of a farmer discussing how he treats possibly rabid livestock.

A distinction must be drawn between Eastern State's inaugural few decades and the years that followed. Built to house 250 prisoners, between 1829 and 1846, 2,176 prisoners passed in and out of the penitentiary (some of whom were women—all of whom were housed in cellblock 7). As the prison population grew, the state of Pennsylvania simply paid to increase ESP's size, adding additional cellblocks and eventually building not only out, but up, thereby destroying the skylights featured in Haviland's original design. Management seemed adamant that the "separate system" should remain in effect for as long as the building would allow.

As the penitentiary grew, so, too, did reports concerning inhumane treatment of its prisoners. It seems that the guards, sure-footed in their socked feet, were not only sneaking around the facility, spying on inmates through feeding holes, but they were also brutalizing the men they were paid to oversee. As Susan Hutchison Tassin stated, "paranoia among prisoners was rampant and well founded." In addition to the shower bath, guards also had the option of placing an unruly (or merely unlikable) prisoner in an "iron gag." This contraption was a "five inch piece of metal, somewhat resembling a horse bit, that was placed over the prisoner's tongue." Once the gag was put inside of the prisoner's mouth, his arms were brought behind his back, tied together, and pulled up towards his head, so that his wrists could be affixed to the gag. It did not take long for a prisoner, contorted in this manner, to learn that struggling deepened the gag.

It is not surprising then, that an 1897 article published in the *Philadelphia Inquirer* stated that "the stories that are told of convicts . . . are heart rendering in the extreme. Such brutality reminds one of the Middle Ages." This reported brutality echoes Dickens' belief the place was inhumane. "The system here," Dickens had written, "is rigid, strict, and hopeless solitary confinement. I believe it, in its effects, to be cruel and wrong. I hold this slow, and daily, tampering with the mysteries of the brain to be immeasurably worse than any torture of the body." And, for those inmates who were not deterred by psychological punishment, ESP offered the "Klondike," an underground tomb-like cell where punished prisoners were forced to remain for days on end.

Eventually, change was introduced into prison life. As the Eastern State Penitentiary website acknowledges, "The system of solitary confinement at Eastern State did not so much collapse as erode away over the decades. A congregate workshop was added to the complex in 1905, eight years before the Pennsylvania System was officially discontinued. By 1909 an inmate newspaper, the *Umpire,* ran a monthly roster of the inter-Penitentiary baseball league scores."

The early 1900s also saw the penitentiary embracing phrenology, an assessment aimed to determine whether intelligence and criminality could be predicted by the shape and size of one's head. As such, when prisoners were first given their numbers and robes, the prison also created records measuring various parts of a prisoner's face, including the size of his forehead, the width of his cheeks, and the overall size of his nose. Phrenology was a fad that fell out of vogue by the early twentieth century. As the solitary system began to dissolve near the beginning of the 1900s, the operation and environment of the penitentiary had also begun to shift dramatically. As author Paul Kahan describes, "The Pennsylvania System's slow death eroded administrative control over the institution until, by the 1920s, the inmates were quite literally running the asylum."

The Quakers could never ever have anticipated that, by 1920, select inmates would be "offered an opportunity to undergo cosmetic plastic surgery in an attempt to make them seem friendlier and nicer to the society that they had wronged." Perhaps the luckiest inmate at ESP was Albert Lapinsky who, in 1952, underwent a total of eight cosmetic surgeries under the belief that he was an "ugly thief" in need of a "new face." While Lapinsky might have been unattractive, he certainly was charming: All of his surgeries were paid for by funds he collected from fellow inmates.

Once ESP welcomed cohabitation, the penitentiary began to play host to scores of notable characters. In 1929, the (self-proclaimed) "Toughest Man in Philadelphia," William "Blackie" Zupkoski, arrived at the penitentiary, having been sentenced to 70 to 140 years for forty counts of armed robbery. He was not a model prisoner, stabbing an inmate to death during his first year behind bars. Al "Scarface" Capone also served time at Eastern State in

1929; he was locked up for eight months after having been arrested for carrying a concealed weapon. Many believe that Capone actually wanted to be incarcerated to avoid the repercussions of the Saint Valentine's Day Massacre in Chicago. Photos of Capone's ESP cell reveal that his "Park Avenue Block" cell was furnished with rugs, modest furniture, and his own personal radio. Notably, Capone had his tonsils out (for free) while incarcerated at ESP.

Not all Eastern State inmates were so pleased with their accommodations. According to Paul Kahan, in the 1930s "the penitentiary had been criticized . . . for supposedly keeping inmates in luxury, while at the same time the penitentiary was *also* criticized for its purportedly inhumane conditions." Rat infestations were rampant, and riots were frequent.

While scores of prisoners attempted to bolt from Eastern State, arguably the most successful effort came in 1945, when twelve prisoners escaped from the facility, thanks to the craftsmanship of Frederick Tenuto, a Philadelphia mob hit man. Using the most rudimentary equipment, Tenuto whittled a narrow tunnel that, in spaces, was only eighteen inches in circumference. The chute successfully allowed for the escape of the dozen men, all of whom were later caught. (It is curious to note that, the following year, Tenuto was transferred to Philadelphia's Holmesburg Prison [see Chapter Ten] where he escaped and was never caught.) Among the escapees was William Francis Sutton, a prolific bank robber otherwise known as the "Gentleman Bandit," who spent a total of eleven years in Eastern State.

By the time mobsters and celebrity thieves arrived at ESP, the prison had become an incredibly different place from the one first imagined by the Quakers. The prison's last major effort to stay modern was the construction of cellblock fifteen— death row—which opened in 1956. This was arguably the final straw in separating the penitentiary from its original purpose: Redemption had finally been replaced by promise of execution.

Eastern State Penitentiary closed in 1971. After a period of inactivity, during which the building sat decaying in the middle of a bustling metropolis, the city of Philadelphia bought the property in 1980. However, it was not until 1994 that ESP was rediscovered as a historic site. The penitentiary is open to the public for guided tours April through December, but its busiest season is, without a doubt, around Halloween. The place is crawling with lost and angry spirits, the voices of those forced to spend hell on earth in Philadelphia.

According to Susan Hutchison Tassin, visitors have "reported seeing shadowy figures darting among the cells, accompanied by a drop in temperature and great feelings of dread. Others say they saw a ghostly figure standing in one of the guard towers. Cell block twelve is generally regarded to be one of the more active paranormally. Visitors sometimes claim they heard the sounds of laughter emanating from some of the cells." The Syfy channel's *Ghost Hunters* have visited the site twice, in 2004 and then again in 2005. The ghost-hunting team (The Atlantic Paranormal Society) saw what they believed to be an apparition in cell block twelve. Multiple members of their squad also admitted to "feelings of dread, heaviness, difficulty breathing" as well as the "hair standing up on the back of [their] necks" and the "feeling of being watched."

While accounts of so-called paranormal activity might seem hokey or entirely fictitious to some, those who had to endure the conditions maintained at the penitentiary argue otherwise. For decades, the inmates who were trapped inside of their cells, and the guards who were held to their posts, were men who had been left entirely alone, comforted only by the voices inside their own heads. While the prisoners are long gone, and their sentences since fulfilled, the legacy of Eastern State Penitentiary is still being carried out by the wretched, restless souls of its past.

# CHAPTER 7

## Unfinished Business: Schuylkill's Molly Maguires

Benjamin Yost was one of two police officers paid to patrol Tamaqua, Pennsylvania. He knew the town well, and was generally respected by the citizens whose safety he sought to uphold. A family man of German descent, he recognized that he was lucky to have a job that wasn't as volatile as the mining work that so many men in the area held. It was really only the miners who caused the trouble that Tamaqua saw—mostly because of their drunken disorderliness, which naturally spiked when they were on strike. In Yost's mind, it wasn't actually the miners who were so lawless, but rather the Molly Maguires—a group of Irish immigrants—whom he knew to be particularly violent. Yost didn't quite know whether he agreed with the "Irish Need Not Apply" signs he saw posted around the area, but he did know that when he arrested James Kerrigan, a Mollie, he usually had to beat him with a club just to gain his compliance. Kerrigan wasn't the only Mollie Yost arrested, but he was arguably the most disreputable. In fact, Yost thought that Kerrigan might be the only man in Eastern Pennsylvania who would think of him as an enemy.

During the first week of June, 1875, Yost was completing his normal patrol which, by two in the morning, involved extinguishing the gas street lamps that dotted the streets of Tamaqua. The way the story was later told, Yost was standing two rungs up his ladder, attempting to dim a lamp directly outside of his home, when two assailants approached and shot him. His wife said that, after hearing the gunshots and her husband's cry, she watched as two shadowy figures fled the scene. She immediately rushed from the house to find her husband bleeding. "Sis, give me a kiss," he is reported to have told her, "I am shot and have to die."

Yost lived for a few more hours; ever devoted to law enforcement, he is said to have used this time to describe his attackers. Yost knew that they weren't local, as he didn't know their names, but he still swore that he had seen them keeping company with local Mollies the day prior. He was also convinced that James Kerrigan must have been somehow involved with his attack.

Before passing away, the policeman remarked to his friends and family, "To think that I served so long in the army, was in so many hard-fought battles, and escaped all the bullets, to die now innocently!" Of those who witnessed his last breaths, eight later testified at the trials held for the five Molly Maguires who were accused of murdering, or plotting to murder, Benjamin Yost.

Those who lived in Eastern Pennsylvania's anthracite coal region knew the Molly Maguires to be Irish immigrants who had come to America for work in the mines. Public perception of the Irish in the United States was generally unforgiving: According to labor leader Sidney Lens, "For a long time the Irish—apart from native Indians, black slaves, and [those of Asian descent]—were the most maltreated ethnic minority in the United States."

The Mollies were thought to have a relationship with the Ancient Order of Hibernians (AOH). This fraternal organization, whose motto was "Friendship, Unity, and Christian Charity," provided aid for the sick and elderly, in addition to serving as a "center for social camaraderie." Groups like the AOH were attractive to immigrants, as such organizations supplied social support from like-minded company. But, for Protestants and other Americans who eschewed the practice of pledging oneself to an organization that operated outside of both church and state, an affiliation with the AOH was tantamount to treason.

In assessing the origins of this distaste for the Irish and, particularly, the Irish immigrants who associated together as the Molly Maguires, we encounter some evidence of fear mongering. As author Kevin Kenny explains in *Making Sense of the Molly Maguires*, "by the late 1850s, the term *Molly Maguires* was being used in the anthracite region as a synonym for Irish social depravity. It was introduced into the political language of the region in 1857 by the nativist editor Benjamin Bannan as a shorthand term for the various aspects of the 'Irish character' he found most objectionable and threatening, including poverty, drunkenness, criminality, insanity, laziness, idolatry, and political corruption."

So, essentially, if you were Irish, spent time with other Irish, and any of you exhibited any negative behaviors, folks would have considered you to be a part of the Molly Maguire crowd.

In the anthracite region of Northeastern Pennsylvania, drama was high, conditions were perilous, and no one knew exactly what being a Molly Maguire entailed. When it came to the Mollies, the hearsay and rumors were rampant. If you polled the locals, they might tell you that the Mollies took part in closed-door meetings where there were secret handshakes and whisky drinks. But, if you asked the men who worked in the coal mines, they'd likely have given a more admiring account of those meetings, as it was an Irishman who spearheaded the first legitimate workers union. The Mollies did not earn the reputation as being associated with (and responsible for) acts of violence until a powerful railroad man needed a group of fall guys.

The man who was so crazed about the Mollies was Franklin B. Gowen, a district attorney-turned-businessman who, by 1870, had become the president of Reading Railroad. At the time he was elected to control the business, Reading was earning capital through the transportation of anthracite coal. But Gowen knew that the real money was in the actual mining of the "black gold." Anthracite coal burns hotter and cleaner than other variants of coal, and sells for two to three times more than other varieties. While the demand for anthracite was high, its supply around the nation was not—it only exists in six counties, all in Eastern Pennsylvania: Schuylkill, Carbon, Lackawanna, Luzerne,

Purported Molly Maguire coffin notice as displayed at Molly Maguire's Pub & Steakhouse, Jim Thorpe, Pennsylvania (www.jimthorpedining.com).

VICTOR A. IZZO

Northumberland, and Columbia. Gowen saw anthracite coal as an opportunity to increase Reading's power and, in turn, fatten his own pockets. Between 1871 and 1874, he purchased 100,000 acres of mining land. Once his company was invested in not only the hauling but also the production of coal, Gowen set out to control the men who worked the mines by acting to thwart those seeking to form labor unions.

The men who worked in the mines had incredibly difficult jobs. Conditions in anthracite mines were extremely dangerous, not to mention "torturously unpleasant" (See Chapter Four for more about mining conditions). As labor union historian Sidney Lens detailed, "Working stooped in the bowels of the earth in damp and fetid atmosphere, the miner was subject to all kinds of health hazards—noxious fumes such as 'stink damp' and 'rotten gas,' carbon monoxide, and coal dust which caused bronchial catarrh . . . Tens of thousands of men worked in semi-darkness, knee-deep in water, always in fear of cave-ins and explosions that entombed hundreds each year. Their lot, as one mining clerk put it, was 'little better than semi-slavery.' Hours were long, from dawn to dusk, sanitary conditions impossibly bad." Notably, it wasn't just the men of the anthracite region who were made to battle this underground environment: As this predated any child labor laws, one quarter of the mining work force was composed of children who, as "breaker boys," were paid by miners to separate coal from slate.

For all of this work, the miners brought home a very paltry salary. While children were paid a flat rate each week, adults were paid based on the amount of coal they mined. This amount was far higher than their net wage, however, as each week, the cost of a man's mining supplies, rent for his company-owned home, and the cut he was to pay his breaker boy was deducted from his earnings. Needless to say, when a mining company decided to lower miners' wages, the men panicked. Especially alarmed were the immigrant groups who were utterly reliant on their menial-labor pay, having neither the perceived skill nor the necessary connections to find other work. The Irish were in an especially precarious position, as they were considered "un-hirable" by many Americans.

Pennsylvania's anthracite region witnessed its first strike in 1842. It was followed by another one in 1849, organized by John

Bates and the "Bates Union," when miners demanded that their salaries be paid in cash, as opposed to being offered as credit at the company store. The Bates Union did not have a particularly large membership, and like many other fledging start-ups across the country, its legacy was short.

It was not until the emergence of John Siney, an Irish immigrant who, while not a particularly skilled laborer, possessed the gift of charisma, that the first regional labor union formed. Under Siney's leadership, the Workingmen's Benevolent Association (WBA) was created; by 1870, the union had thirty thousand members, a majority of whom were from Pennsylvania's anthracite region. While these numbers were relatively small, Siney was able to earn Pennsylvania's miners sliding-scale pay (so that their wages increased as the price of coal rose) and encourage the state legislature to pass a vote approving the right for working people to "form societies, and associations for their mutual aid, benefit, and protection." Over time, there seemed to be legitimate promise in the WBA's prospective ability to protect mining men and their families.

Unsurprisingly, Reading Railroad's Gowen feared the progress being made by the WBA, as any organized labor forces threatened to decrease the profit Reading sought to make in its mines. So, to instigate a reaction, in 1871 Gowen saw to it that miners' wages were cut by one-third. The miners naturally initiated a strike, and the entire anthracite region was thrown into a collective concern: Men worried that their families would starve, while independent contractors feared that, without workers, their livelihoods, too, would disappear. Gowen dared contractors to hire blacklegs (strikebreakers) by increasing the cost of his railroad's freight rates; this move assured that, even if the strikebreakers were able to produce a product, the contractors couldn't afford to haul it. A man of discernible influence, Gowen quickly convinced all railroads operating in the area to also increase their fares, crippling the mining industry altogether. The savvy yet unscrupulous move heightened concern in the area, causing the Harrisburg *State Journal* to declare that, "If a railroad company can advance and lower its charges for transportation at will, there is not an industrial operation that may not be destroyed in a month." The strikers were forced to abandon their cause and return to work, accepting an arbitrator's decision to lower minimum wages by fifty cents to a measly $2.50.

Gowen was no idiot. When state legislators began to look into objections raised by the WBA, he created a diversion by announcing that there was a criminal organization embedded within the WBA. Fingering the Mollies, Gowen coyly outlined, "I say there is an association which votes in secret, at night, that men's lives shall be taken, and they shall be shot before their wives, murdered in cold blood . . . it happens that the only men who are shot are the men who dare to disobey the mandates of the Workingmen's Benevolent Association." In making this proclamation, Gowen took himself out of the public eye. On top of this, he also publically implicated the Molly Maguires as being a criminal organization that was responsible for any unsolved violence that had occurred in Pennsylvania's anthracite region.

It is certain that a number of mining superintendents had been murdered during the mid-to-late 1800s. The crimes, unsolved by the tiny police forces employed in the area, appeared to be driven by labor unrest. One foreman who was killed was known for "short-weighing" miners' output, thereby consistently underpaying all of the men who worked during his shift. But, thanks to Gowen's suggestion that there was vengeful criminality afoot, many began to believe rumors that the violence was not the work of ordinary miners, but rather the targeted work of those plotting, murderous, Molly Maguires. As author John T. Morse Jr., a contemporary of the Mollies, asserted, "Everywhere and at all times [superintendents and bosses] were attacked, beaten, and shot down, by day and by night; month after month and year after year, on the public highways and in their own homes, in solitary places and in the neighborhood of crowds these doomed men continued to fall in frightful succession." It somehow felt better to believe that these men were killed not because they had knowingly wronged their workers, but rather because they were victims of gang violence.

Soon enough, people began to believe Gowen's declaration. Townsfolk were telling stories that the Mollies were using regular AOH meetings to plot the deaths of those bosses who underpaid them, who gave them harder assignments, or whom a Mollie simply didn't like. And, during times of strikes, stories surfaced that the Mollies were also targeting blacklegs. As per the reported Mollie code, the mark of the group's ire was not ambushed or spontaneously beaten. Instead, the man would receive a "coffin notice," which served as a death warrant, naming the Mollie's terms of settlement, often accompanied by drawings of pistols and coffins. The following note was reportedly written by a Mollie's hand: "Mr. John Taylor—Please leave Glen Carbon or if you don't you will suffer . . . WE will give you one week to go but if you are alive on next Saturday you will die. Remember and leave."

The year 1873 played host to many big changes in the anthracite region. John Siney had been appointed the president of a new union, the Miners' National Association, whose pronounced goal was to prompt arbitrations as opposed to strikes. Meanwhile, as the Molly Maguires were allegedly meeting in secret, scripting violence, Franklin Gowen called a confidential meeting of his own in New York between the heads of the big railroads. By the meeting's end, the five largest railroads (the Reading, the Hudson, the Jersey-Central, the Lackawanna, and the Pennsylvania Coal Company) had divided the market between themselves, celebrating the lack of any American antitrust laws to prohibit such a blanketed partnership.

But Gowen's hold on the region did not stop with controlling its primary commerce; he also began to make bigger moves to control his largest threat—the miner's union. After his East Coast meeting, Gowen traveled to Chicago to meet with Allan Pinkerton, who ran a detective agency (the agency later served as the model for the FBI, created in 1908). It was Gowen's plan to have Pinkerton help destroy the growing mining union and, more specifically, the Molly Maguires. Pinkerton and his people were familiar with Eastern Pennsylvania, having been employed by various railroad, mining, and iron companies as a private Coal and Iron Police force since 1865. Upon Gowen's request, Pinkerton deployed James McParlan, an Irish Catholic, to Schuylkill, Pennsylvania.

According to many historians, it was Gowen's plan for McParlan to infiltrate and then take down the Molly Maguires, exposing them as the terrorists that everyone knew them to be. However, Ancient Order of Hibernians history—as recorded by Sidney Lens—contends that Gowen's motives were much more nefarious. "Gowen, the AOH said, wanted an informer who would simultaneously insinuate himself into the Mollies 'and become its leader.' As its new head, he would be expected to provoke strikes; have his men kill mine bosses; murder English, Welsh, and German miners; and generally cause so much trouble that 'the collieries (mines) will be unable to run for want of competent men.' In the ensuing chaos, independent operators would have to sell their holdings to the Reading at depreciated prices." While Gowen's exact motives are up for debate, it is clear that, in hiring a Pinkerton detective, his aim was to destroy the Molly Maguires. In order to ward off corruption (Pinkerton's detectives were lauded for being above corruption), it was agreed that Gowen would pay McParlan twelve dollars per week, regardless of what or how much dirt he was able to dredge up on the Mollies.

James McParlan moved to Pennsylvania in the fall of 1873, and joined the Mollies under the name James McKenna. The detective, thirty years old and redheaded, was welcomed into the AOH, eventually securing a spot at many of the Mollie's closed-door meetings. Not a miner by trade, McParlan said he was a murderer and counterfeiter who was on the run from authorities; he reportedly won over his Irish countrymen based on both his charm and his saloon readiness. It should be noted that all of what is known about McParlan's activity as a Mollie was recorded by the detective himself.

While James McKenna was busily drinking and plotting with the Mollies, Franklin Gowen was readying the coal industry for yet another strike. In 1875 it was announced that wages would be cut by between 10 and 20 percent, and that the minimum wage would no longer hold steady at $2.50. But Gowen's hand in the strike did not end here: He also reportedly employed two additional Pinkerton detectives, Robert Linden and W. J. Heisler, paying them to protect blacklegs, and to assault striking miners. The violence quickly reached a new peak. Strikers were killing strikebreakers while Gowen's paid "vigilance committee" attacked union men and "striker activists." All the while, the region suffered as everyone in the mining community struggled simply to get by.

A legitimate tally of the violence reveals that "there was much more terror waged against the Mollies than those . . .

Irishmen ever aroused." However, historical accounts from 1875 regarding the strike reveal that, at the time, most citizens were all too willing to blame the Molly Maguires for the violence that erupted in the area. Unsurprisingly, when, after five months, the starving miners agreed to Gowen's proposed 20-percent wage cut and his refusal to work with union mines, everybody was looking for someone to blame for the debacle. As lamented by Sidney Lens, in the wake of Gowen's victory, the Molly Maguires were goners: "The Mollies, hailed and bloated in scores of newspaper stories, were a made-to-order scapegoat —'it was sufficient to hang a man,' the railroad president himself admitted, 'to declare him a Molly Maguire.'"

Following a rash of violence, including the murder of Benjamin Yost, twenty Mollies were arrested by the Coal and Iron Police and charged with vicious crimes against members of the community. While it was initially anticipated that he would not have to participate in any legal proceedings, James McParlan testified at multiple trials, each resulting in the imprisonment or death of the accused Mollie. One Mollie, James "Powder Keg" Kerrigan, turned state's evidence and testified against his brothers; following the trials he was given the nickname "The Squealer" and spent the rest of his life in exile in Virginia.

There was considerable drama surrounding the testimony offered by both the undercover detective and Mollie-turned-traitor. But, without a doubt, the most outstanding component of the Molly Maguire trials was the participation of Franklin

Gowen himself. Gowen, thanks to his experience as Schuylkill County's District Attorney (serving between 1862–1864), inserted himself in the trials by shelling out one hundred thousand dollars to cover their proceedings. He also served as the prosecutor for the case. During the trial, Gowen posited that the Molly Maguires were among the most terrifying of any criminals known to man: "Search the pages of history and go back over the records of the world, and I will venture to say you will never find in any society, claiming to be civilized, such an adjudication to death, and by instruments of vengeance as ghastly and as horrible, as this society wielded for the murder of their fellow men."

Strikingly, as noted by historian Anthony F. C. Wallace, neither McParlan nor Kerrigan—the prosecution's main witnesses—gave evidence to corroborate this image of the Mollies as monsters. In fact, "The reports and testimony of McParlan do not reveal a gang of professional criminals planning bank and train robberies, extorting protection money from collieries, smuggling liquor, or kidnapping for ransom. There were no rapes or beatings of women. Members showed some participation in the political process as Democrats, much of it quite irregular, with the aim of advancing local interests of the Irish. There was no AOH involvement in union activity at all." Even still, Gowen played on the palpable need to punish someone for the chaos of the region, as he deftly attributed area violence to the Molly Maguires.

Ten of the Mollies sent to the gallows died on the same day: June 21, 1877 was henceforth referred to as either "Black Thursday" or "The Day of the Rope." The most notable Mollie to die was John "Black Jack" Kehoe, who was considered by many to be the "King of the Mollies." Kehoe, having once served as the county delegate (the highest officer of the AOH), died on December 18, 1878, for the murder of mine superintendent F. W. Langdon in 1862. As he was the last of the Mollies to die, Kehoe's death marks what many consider to be the "death of Molly-ism."

Were the Molly Maguires vigilantes or scapegoats? Were they ruthless murderers or champions of labor unions? The lasting reputation of these Pennsylvanians should be less about the fear these supposed Irish villains evoked, and more about the injustice the anthracite region suffered at the hands of Gowen's limitless power. As historian Harold Aurand notes, the Molly Maguire trials are "one of the most astounding surrenders of sovereignty in American history. A private corporation initiated the investigation through a private detective agency; a private police force arrested the alleged offenders; the coal company attorneys prosecuted them. The state only provided the courtroom and hangman." Perhaps the only justice that could have been served occurred on December 14, 1889, when Franklin B. Gowen died thanks to a bullet wound to his head. Gowen was found alone in a Washington, DC, hotel room. According to reports, at the time of Gowen's death there were no known witnesses, and not a Mollie in sight.

# CHAPTER 8

## *Unfinished Business: Lancaster's Paxton Boys*

It all began on Wednesday, the 14th of December, 1763. It was dark, but not so dark that you couldn't see the snow and sleet catching onto the coats of those who had gathered in front of Matthew Smith and Lazarus Stewart. Those congregating tried not to shift their feet, or sniffle, or show any sign of weakness. At that very moment, only Smith and Stewart held the bravado that the men needed to conjure, or at the very least, hoped to fake. The crew of fifty-seven was soon to take matters into their own hands and begin what would later be known as the Conestoga Massacre.

It is uncertain whether the men crept to the Conestoga camp, or if they marched loudly, talking at volumes that seemed neither suspicious nor obvious. The Conestogas lived quietly in the frontier, having established an agreement of "peace and amity" with their white neighbors dating back to when King Charles chartered the land to William Penn in 1681. But the

Paxton Boys' mission had nothing to do with this precedent of peace. Their visit was one prompted by malice and executed with premeditation.

After riding through the night, the Paxton Boys arrived at the Indian camp enough after daybreak that some of the Conestogas were already elsewhere, selling their handmade wares to nearby settlers. The only known witness to the atrocities that took place at the camp was a young boy who fled the scene during the attack. Later, when writing about the massacre, leader Matthew Smith noted, "We met, and our party, under cover of the night, rode off for Conestogue. Our plan was well laid; the scout who had traced the Indians was with us; the village was stormed and reduced to ashes."

It has been recorded that, later on the 14th, the Paxton Boys were seen with bloody tomahawks dangling from the saddles of their horses. It was also reported that, soon after murdering the Conestogas, they were overheard, in a nearby town, asking about the repercussions of "killing Indians."

The first responders to the Conestoga town found six dead, including Shehaes, a chief who had been born on the land and was known for fostering the tribe's positive relationship with neighboring whites. Members of Shehaes's family were also victimized, although we have no understanding of who was made to watch whom die. As Benjamin Franklin would later write in his 1764 account of the massacre, "These poor defenceless [*sic*] Creatures were immediately fired upon, stabbed and hatcheted [*sic*] to Death! The good Shehaes among the rest, cut to Pieces in his Bed. All of them were scalped, and otherwise horribly mangled. Then their Huts were set on Fire, and most of them burnt down." Franklin was not alone in his horror: In the days following the massacre, reverberations of the Conestogas' deaths would be felt seventy miles west in Philadelphia.

After the slaughter, there were only fourteen remaining members of the Conestoga tribe. A few of the Conestogas decided to travel to the nearby town of Lancaster, where they were immediately given refuge. In fact, the concern for the remaining Conestogas' safety was so high that magistrates actually sent for those natives who did not voluntarily seek asylum. Soon enough, all of the remaining members of the Conestoga tribe were living in a Lancaster workhouse—the best-protected facility in town—under the watchful protection of white settlers.

The fact that the settlers were so concerned with the safety of the remaining Conestogas reveals two key insights into what life was like out on the Pennsylvania frontier. First, thanks to the legacy established by William Penn, who had provided the Conestogas safe land in the 1690s, there was a true harmony that existed between this tribe of Native Americans and their white neighbors. Many of the settlers in the area were Quakers who opposed any form of violence. Beyond this, the Natives were hardly threatening, as they were small in number and lacking both aid and hostility. It is said that the Conestoga children made easy friends with their white counterparts and, in turn, the whites welcomed the Conestogas onto their property and into their homes. This mutually respectful relationship even resulted in many Indian children being named after their parents' favorite white neighbors.

Second, although this was the first act of vigilante violence carried out by the Paxton Boys (also referred to as the Paxton Rangers), based on the gruesome nature of the December 14th attack, immediately after the incident their contemporaries had begun to fear what the Boys would do next. Certainly, any group willing to kill off Shehaes—described by Benjamin Franklin as being "an exceeding good man, considering his education; being naturally of a most kind, benevolent temper"—could be trusted to commit more atrocities.

The Paxton Rangers came together relatively inauspiciously. Their original members were predominately Irish or Ulster Scots; they were a group of frontiersmen, many of whom had fought in both the French and Indian and Pontiac's Wars, all living in, or close to, the township of Dauphin (then called Paxtang). These immigrant settlers self-identified as faithful Presbyterians and ex-soldiers who distrusted neighboring Indian tribes, many of whom they had fought as enemies during the French and Indian War.

In towns such as Lancaster, deep hostilities continued after the war, especially between the men who fought as soldiers and the Indians who ultimately lost the battle to keep their land. As reported by the Historical Society of Pennsylvania in 1860, "A letter from Paxton . . . says, that 'a woman was roasted, and had two hinges in her hands, supposed to be put in red hot, and several of the men had awls thrust into their eyes, and spears, arrows and pitchforks sticking in their bodies.' [A Colonial] stated that two thousand persons had been killed or carried off by the Indians, and some thousands driven to beggary and distress." It goes without saying that the end of the war did not entirely quell the animosity simmering between the two factions.

Many credit ex-soldiers Matthew Smith and Lazarus Stewart as being the founders of the Paxton Boys. Smith was an early settler in Paxton who was described by others as good looking, illiterate, and "outrageously talkative." According to some, he was also frequently "in the liquor" and not much of a solider as a result. Stewart, on the other hand, was known to be a "dangerous villain" who was considered to be the violent, de facto ringleader of the Rangers.

Lazarus Stewart spared no detail when accounting for his personal hatred of the Natives: "The bloody barbarians had exercised on our fathers, mothers, brothers, sisters, wives, and children and relatives, the most unnatural and leisurely tortures; butchered others in their beds, at their meals, or in some unguarded hour. Our people recalled to their minds, sights of horror, scenes of slaughter; seeing scalps clothed with gore! mangled limbs! women ripped up! the heart and the bowels still palpitating with life, and smoking on the ground! They saw savages swilling the blood of their victims, and imbibing a more courageous fury from the draught. They reasoned thus: These are not men; they are not beasts of prey; they are something worse; they are infernal furies in human shape." Certainly no one would accuse Lazarus of having underutilized his macabre sensibility.

Beyond their animosity toward Native Americans, the men who were drawn to join the Paxton Boys also likely felt alienated from their white society, whose ruling class was shaping up to be suspiciously homogenous. According to historian Alexandra Mancini, although Pennsylvania's Quakers accounted for between one-sixth to one-eighth of the settlement's population, for most of the early 1700s they held a full two-thirds of Pennsylvania's Assembly seats. In some of those years their majority was as high as 90 percent.

Facing the distinct possibility of becoming politically irrelevant despite their wartime service, it is understandable that select frontiersmen were beginning to feel disenfranchised. And, in turn, it is reasonable that, coupled with their residual animosity from the French and Indian and Pontiac's Wars, there was a sense of collective hostility. So what did the Paxton Boys do? Like any predictable group of bullies, they chose to pick on the one group over whom they could wield the greatest power: the twenty-two remaining members of the peaceful Conestoga community.

In a move to appoint themselves vigilantes (as opposed to standard frontier murderers), the Paxtons created a story that they could use to justify their attack on the Natives. According to the Rangers' retrofitted version of events, the Conestogas were violent. The Boys claimed that a Native who was sympathetic to their cause had fingered Will Sock, a Conestoga, as being responsible for killing multiple (unnamed) white settlers. To substantiate Sock's disreputable status, a handful of prominent Lancaster residents attested to having heard him make ominous threats, in addition to seeing him "acting suspiciously." Others stated that Sock was not only a killer, but he was also harboring other like-minded murderers. The case was therefore made that the Conestogas must suffer a violent end.

The colloquial testimony gathered regarding Sock's menacing nature was paltry, if not obviously fabricated. Even so, the Paxton Rangers were able to effectively spread their propaganda. As reported by the Historical Society of Pennsylvania in 1860, "It was commonly believed, on the border, that the Indians who were murdering every unprotected man, woman and child, plundering and burning every thing they could lay hands upon, were concealed by these Conestogas and that they acted as their spies." Or at least this is what the Paxtons wanted their friends and neighbors to believe.

Available literature suggests that the slaughter committed on the 14th of December actually roused immediate sympathy in the white, Quaker communities surrounding Paxtang. As Quaker Robert Proud wrote, the Paxtons "committed the most horrible massacre, that ever was heard of in this, or perhaps, any other province, with impunity . . . [by] murder[ing] the remains of a whole tribe of peaceable, inoffensive, helpless Indians, who were

British subjects, young and old, men, women and children." The support for the Native Americans stretched as far as Philadelphia, where, within five days of the Paxton Boys' attack, Governor John Penn (William's grandson) requested that a warrant be issued for the Paxtons' arrest and offered a reward for their capture. When a warrant was not expedited, on December 22, Penn began encouraging citizens of Pennsylvania to locate and confront the Rangers themselves. However, as the Historical Society of Pennsylvania was quick to point out, "Their arrest . . . was impossible, without arresting the whole frontier." The Paxtons were a well-protected group.

It is unclear what, if any, attempts were made to corral the vigilante squad following their initial attack on the Conestogas. There is an equal dearth of information regarding what, specifically, the Paxton Boys were up to following their initial slaughter of the Conestogas. They stayed hidden for thirteen days; however, when they did reappear, there was no question that they were still committed to their cause.

On December 27, 1763, the determined Rangers entered Lancaster on horseback. Over one hundred strong, they were now larger in number and brazenly energized by their expanding muscle. Someone had tipped the Paxton Boys off to the Conestoga's whereabouts and, due to their volume and strength, the workhouse setting did little to deter the determined gang as they set out to finish off the tribe in full.

As I. S. Clare wrote in 1892, "The murderers did their work with rifles, tomahawks and scalping-knives. The victims were horribly butchered, some having their brains blown out, others their legs chopped off, others their hands cut off. Bill Sock and his wife Molly and their two children had their heads split open and scalped. The other victims were John Smith and his wife Peggy, Captain John and his wife Betty and their son Little John, the little boys Jacob, Christy and Little Peter, and Peggy and another little girl."

Some reports suggest that the Paxtons were successful in extinguishing all of the Conestogas, while other sources say that two tribe members were able to escape. In 2005, Jessie Marafioti, a Native American who claimed to have heard the story of the attack from her grandmother, published her own version of the Lancaster massacre. According to Marafioti, the Conestogas were not in the workhouse when they were surrounded and killed but, rather, the massacre occurred while they were worshipping at a Lancaster church. Marafioti contends that her ancestors recited the Lord's Prayer as they were murdered. In response, the Paxton Boys were reported to have accused, "You lying heathens!" "What makes you think Jesus wants to hear your prayers?" and "The only good Indian is a dead one."

While Marafioti expressed her desire to tell of the massacre from a Native American perspective (something that is notably lacking in our present-day understanding of life on the frontier) Lancaster historian James Stokes questions the credibility of Marafioti's story, stating that there was no church near the workhouse where the Conestogas were being housed.

As is often the case with the retelling of historic horror, many accounts of the eradication of the Conestoga tribe are plagued with overwrought emotion. Take, for example, Benjamin Franklin's recorded thoughts regarding the Lancaster attack:

> The barbarous Men who committed the atrocious act, in Defiance of Government, of all Laws human and divine, and to the eternal Disgrace of their Country and Colour, then mounted their Horses, huzza'd in Triumph, as if they had gained a Victory, and rode off—unmolested!
>
> The Bodies of the Murdered were then brought out and exposed in the Street, till a Hole could be made in the Earth, to receive and cover them. But the Wickedness cannot be covered, the Guilt will lie on the whole Land, till Justice is done on the Murderers. THE BLOOD OF THE INNOCENT WILL CRY TO HEAVEN FOR VENGEANCE.

The Paxton Boys did not turn around and go home after their killing spree in Lancaster. Instead, following their assault on the Conestogas, they rode east to attack the Moravian Indians, whom they believed were responsible for the murder of some traveling Scotsmen several months prior. Arriving in Philadelphia, the Paxtons were met by not only the Moravians, but also groups of Quakers who announced their unprecedented willingness to act in the Native Americans' defense. After a tense stand-off, during which Benjamin Franklin served as a representative for the Quakers and, in turn, the Moravians, the Paxton Rangers agreed to return home if Pennsylvania lawmakers agreed to hear their complaints about political underrepresentation.

At this moment, the Paxton Boys became engaged in not only a standoff with Philadelphia lawmakers, but also with the very traditions upon which Pennsylvania was founded. As posited by a number of historians, including Kevin Kenny and Alexandra Mancini, the ideology of the Paxton Boys was in direct odds with that of Pennsylvania's founder, William Penn. While Penn was compelled to extend neighborly respect to the Native Americans who inhabited the land prior to his purchase of the acreage, the Paxton's philosophy was more aligned with John Locke's belief in private property (although Locke did not advocate Paxton-style violence). The Paxton's "logic of displacement" was therefore emblematic of a petition that was only just beginning to emerge in America: the expression of "a desperate desire for land and safety during wartime." The Paxtons began documenting their grievances and distributing them to others by way of pamphlet.

Therefore, while their actions were abhorrent and their victims defenseless, the Paxton Rangers were acting from a very real and powerless position. As Mancini reasons, "Like the backcountry inhabitants of other colonial regions, Pennsylvania backcountry settlers felt neglected and alienated; they distrusted the motives of the urban elite; and felt totally unable to improve their situation because they were unequally represented. The

Paxton *Declaration and Remonstrance* summarized these senti-
ments when the frontiersmen claimed that they were 'a People
grossly abused, unrighteously burdened and made Dupes,' and
when they pleaded for the rescue of 'a labouring Land from a
Weight so oppressive, unreasonable and unjust.'"

At the moment that they laid down their weapons and
picked up their pens, the Paxton Boys engaged in what Murray N. Rothbard deemed a "furious pamphlet war." That war,
waged between the Quaker (and pro-Quaker) contingent and
the Paxtons (acting as representatives of Irish and Scottish frontiersmen), certainly "reflected the institutional weaknesses in
Pennsylvania." It might have also "paved the way for internal
revolution" in America.

None of the Paxton Boys were successfully arrested (Lazarus Stewart evaded three arrest attempts) and none were ever
prosecuted for their roles in having gruesomely eliminated the
Conestogas. While some, like Kevin Kenny and Alexandra
Mancini, have made efforts to recognize that the Paxtons were,
at least in part, motivated by political discontent, it should be
noted that Pennsylvania does not play host to any Paxton Boys
statues. Instead, it is the Conestogas who are rightfully honored
in and around the state. Go to Conestoga Indian Town or Lancaster and you will see thoughtful memorials, recognizing how
the Conestogas' peaceful way of life was brought to a tragic end
thanks at the hands of the ruthless Paxton Boys.

# CHAPTER 9

# *Unclear Intentions:*
# *Philadelphia's Dr. Albert Kligman*

I f walls hold secrets, prison cells hold lifetimes. Within Philadelphia's Holmesburg Prison, men existed as best they could: Some got into trouble and extended their stay, while others kept to themselves whenever possible. The mess hall and common corridors were overrun with danger, and like so many things in America, leaving this bad situation took a combination of cash and savvy. Fortunately for some, between 1951 and 1974, Holmesburg's prisoners were given a reliable way to make money. During these two decades, inmates had hundreds of chances to sacrifice their skin and bodies and, at times, their minds, to the clinical tests and experimentations being run by University of Pennsylvania dermatologist Albert M. Kligman.

In describing Kligman's "milkshake test," William Robb, an inmate serving a life sentence for murder, explained to author Allen M. Hornblum, how "each day selected inmates went to H Block and drank 'a rich, creamy-tasting 'milkshake,' something like today's diet drinks. The test lasted anywhere from thirty to ninety days depending on the results [from] each . . . inmate. Two types of milkshakes were given out to the inmates: a vanilla-flavored concoction for the thinnies and a chocolate-flavored one for the fatties. . . . At first, [there was] a problem with the milkshake test: The first three weeks, the fatties gained weight and the thinnies lost weight and suffered dehydration. There was a mix-up . . . where the milkshakes were being passed out. . . . It took a while for the lab to work out the bugs."

Robb's description of the milkshake test is telling for a handful of reasons. First, it highlights a reasonable span of time during which the medical trials often lasted; second, it evidences that Kligman—a dermatologist—was running experiments that had very little to do with his field of training; and third, it depicts the University of Pennsylvania's lab as being run extremely slop-pily. But we're getting ahead of ourselves by skipping to Klig-man's errors before we even know how he got his foot in the door. To begin, let's get a lay of the land.

Before it closed in 1995, most of the men who were being held in Philadelphia's Holmesburg Prison were awaiting their sentencing, uncertain of how long they would be incarcerated. As they waited, four, possibly even five men were crowded into a six-by-eight-foot cell; these cramped units were described as nothing short of pigsties. Rape was common, and jobs were scarce. And, by mid-century, the prison was still reeling from the 1938 "bake-oven deaths," when four prisoners who were striking against the prison's meal system were killed after guards locked them in an enclosed room and then cranked up the heat. To state the obvious: Life in Philadelphia's Holmesburg Prison was hellish.

Most Holmesburg men didn't have family or friends in the free world who were able to hire an attorney or make bail for them, so they spent their time behind bars focused on staying alive and hoarding whatever cash came their way. A shop worker at Holmesburg made anywhere from between fifteen to twenty-five cents an hour; this was not a job to scoff at, however, as over half of the prisoners at Holmesburg were unable to secure any form of employment.

Enter 1951 and Dr. Albert M. Kligman, the University of Pennsylvania dermatologist responsible for altering the financial landscape of the jail. Kligman was initially invited to Holmesburg to assess and hopefully curtail a rampant outbreak of athlete's foot. But, upon touring the facilities, he was immediately struck with the immense potential housed within the prison's gated walls. As Kligman later told a reporter with Philadelphia's *Evening Bulletin:* "All I saw before me were acres of skin. It was like a farmer seeing a fertile field for the first time."

In the early 1950s, Kligman was relatively new to the field of research. Born in Philadelphia in 1916, Kligman earned a bachelor's degree at Penn State University in 1939 and followed this with a doctorate in botany from the University of Pennsylvania in 1942; five years later, at the urging of his first wife, he earned his medical degree from Penn. Having studied fungi as a botanist, Kligman decided to focus his medical career on dermatology. Many would later contend that, with Kligman's unchecked enthusiasm and the national recognition he brought to the University of Pennsylvania, Kligman was personally responsible for elevating dermatology from "pimple-popping" to a highly relevant field. But, it seems that those captivated by Kligman's charm made little effort to assess his scruples.

Kligman's first sanctioned research concerned ringworm (the fungus responsible for athlete's foot), and his test subjects were institutionalized children with mental disabilities. As his colleague Dr. Margaret Grey Wood would later tell it, Albert Kligman was not particularly sensitive when it came to his research subjects. Rather, he was quick to laugh over how easy it was to compel their participation, having made such remarks as, "These kids want attention so bad, if you hit them over the head with a hammer they would love you for it."

Although the prisoners he encountered at Holmesburg certainly had more street smarts than his previous subjects, Kligman was able to easily make the transition from working with the institutionalized to the incarcerated when he set up shop at Holmesburg. His first years were inarguably productive, despite the fact that his working relationship with the prison and its superintendent was suspiciously informal. Years later Kligman would brag to a colleague, "I began to go to the prison regularly, although I had no authorization. It was years before the authorities knew that I was conducting various studies on prisoner volunteers. Things were simpler then. Informed consent was unheard of. No one asked me what I was doing. It was a wonderful time."

Now would be a good time to pause to situate Albert Kligman and his research within the context of American medicine.
As a doctor, Kligman was required to follow the Hippocratic
Oath which, in part, notes "I will come for the benefit of the
sick, remaining free of all intentional injustice, of all mischief."
As Kligman defined his ideal professional setting as being steeped
in secrecy, thus offering him a total lack of accountability, it
seems reasonable to conclude that Kligman was unconcerned
with whether he was doing right by his patients. In fact, he also
appeared unconcerned with the tenets of the Nuremberg Code.
Created in reaction to discovery that doctors in Nazi Germany
were conducting medical experiments on individuals kept in
concentration camps, the Code was written in 1947 for the
expressed purpose of defining informed consent.

Within its ten main points, the Code mandates that: "voluntary consent of the human subject is absolutely essential"; "no
experiment should be conducted where there is a prior reason to
believe that death or disabling injury will occur; except, perhaps,
in those experiments where the experimental physicians also
serve as subjects"; "the experiment should be conducted only by
scientifically qualified persons. The highest degree of skill and
care should be required through all stages of the experiment of
those who conduct or engage in the experiment"; and, perhaps
most relevant to Kligman and his research, "the degree of risk to
be taken should never exceed that determined by the humanitarian importance of the problem to be solved by the experiment."
The Nuremberg Code was in effect when Kligman took the

Hippocratic Oath, and it most certainly was in effect when he first began at Holmesburg. Even still, he held a complete disregard for the practice of or principle behind informed consent. It should come as no surprise, then, that when we start assessing the particulars of Kligman's research, the lack of informed consent is only the beginning of his professional transgressions.

Over his twenty years at Holmesburg, Kligman ran hundreds of studies for a handful of pharmaceutical companies as well as for the US Army and possibly even the CIA. He was paid handsomely for his services, reportedly only splitting a leftover sum between his technicians, subjects, Holmesburg Prison, and his primary employer, the University of Pennsylvania. Due to the nature of his research, in addition to having to answer to both the prison and Penn in order to run tests, Dr. Kligman also regularly had to seek approval from the Food and Drug Administration and, after its establishment in the 1970s, the Environmental Protection Agency. And, had it not been stocked full of his friends—none of whom recalled ever meeting to discuss his Holmesburg research—the Institutional Review Board that reviewed Kligman's work would also have proven to be a legitimate source of oversight.

Despite, or perhaps because of, his having to answer to a host of overseers, Kligman kept extremely paltry records to evidence the particulars of his research. Lists of volunteering prisoners were frequently misplaced or destroyed, research protocols were full of holes, and dosages were haphazardly measured: In short, reliable accountability was an utter impossibility. This lack of culpability has since permitted members of Kligman's

Holmesburg staff to disavow their knowledge of and involvement in his research.

Despite the lack of paperwork and professional ownership, attorneys and journalists have found some success in piecing together elements of Kligman's research, thanks to the Freedom of Information Law and statements from Holmesburg prisoners themselves. What they've found is startling.

One component to Dr. Kligman's research protocol was his reliance on prisoners and other untrained staff to assist him in administering the trials to subjects. Al Zabala, an ex-inmate, recounted to author Allen M. Hornblum the amateur nature of early Holmesburg trials: "We were given jars marked A, B, C, D . . . with percentages of 2 percent, 8 percent, 4 percent. . . . We had to mix the creams together and then put them on the inmates. This one time, I got the job to mix the chemicals for the test, and I wasn't paying attention to what I was doing. But I still had the sense to test it on myself [before I used it] and it burned a hole the size of a thumbnail in my right forearm. It hurt like hell. If I [had] put that stuff on an inmate, he would have come back at me with a pipe or a shank."

Another mainstay of Kligman's research was his habit of abandoning trials midway through the test if preliminary results did not match his anticipated or desired result. While his apparent unwillingness to carry out unsuccessful trials could be attributable to his desire to please the big pharmaceutical companies who were paying him to gain FDA approval of their products, it might also have had something to do with the fact that Kligman lacked training as a clinician.

While it might seem illogical for a doctor whose research techniques were so messy and background so undernourished to have secured contracts with large companies like Johnson & Johnson and the Dow Chemical Company, it is important to keep in mind that one of the primary benefits of Kligman's protocol was that his research was cheap. The meager money the inmates received from the University of Pennsylvania would never have given way to statistically significant recruitment or participation of human subjects in the outside world. But, according to the prisoners who signed up for his studies, the payment was better than anything else available to them at the time.

Jack Lopinson, a Holmesburg Prison alum, admitted to Allen Hornblum, "The biggest reason guys went into the [research program was that] drug tests were the best-paying jobs. Prison [labor] didn't pay and here was easy money." With money, a prisoner could send funds to his family, hire an attorney, bribe or pay off other prisoners, or use it to buy cigarettes, candy, or cookies. While the effects of the money might have been "disastrous," as then Assistant District Attorney Alan J. Davis argued, in real time the prisoners were all too eager to turn their bodies over to science for quick and steady paychecks.

Through Kligman's clinical trials, inmates were presented with hundreds of opportunities to earn cash by surrendering themselves as guinea pigs to test anything from lipstick, suntan lotion, deodorant, and weight-loss shakes to prospective chemical weapons and possibly toxic drugs. One popular test at Holmesburg was the "patch test," which required inmates to have a grid created on their back, made from hospital tape.

As inmate William Robb explained to author Allen M. Hornblum, "The grid consisted of about twenty squares. In each one of these squares, a dab of lotion was applied, and the inmate's back was exposed to different temperatures from a sunlamp. The exposure to the sunlamp lasted anywhere from fifteen to thirty minutes, after which each square was inspected for degree of blistering or other adverse reactions. . . . The grid was then covered with a large solid piece of tape (to prevent tampering by the inmate) and the inmate was returned to his cell. This test lasted about thirty days and once a day . . . the inmate was called back over to the lab and exposed to the sunlamp. After about five days of the sunlamp, there [were] sections of the . . . skin that were burnt a deep brown and the skin started to peel, itch, and blister. If a certain square became too damaged it was covered over with a permanent piece of tape and the tests continued on the grid."

Perhaps the milkshake test and the patch test weren't that bad: After all, the prisoners were grown men who were capable of throwing away their milkshakes or removing their grids if desired. Additionally, during his years at Holmesburg, Kligman was also responsible for testing and patenting of Retin-A, a gel that is used to treat acne, pimples, and, if Dr. Kligman was to be believed, wrinkles. These tests—involving food or topical ointments—were relatively low-risk, as they afforded inmates a true opportunity to skew or alter their level of participation. As such, while some believe that Kligman deserves to be shamed for

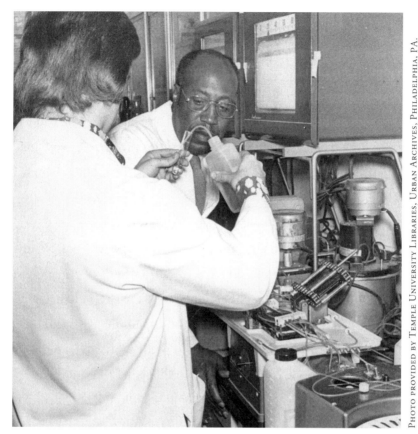

University of Pennsylvania researcher Solomon McBride with a technician in the lab at Holmesburg Prison.

taking advantage of a trapped population by enticing them with scant payment for their services, others see him as simply having provided prisoners with a much-needed source of income that would have otherwise not been made available to them.

This being acknowledged, Kligman should be held responsible for his absolute disregard for the principal of informed consent. Certainly criticism is due when it came to the tests that he was running on unknowing inmates involving the herpes virus and the staphylococcus bacteria. But a much sterner outcry should be made in reaction to the tests he ran at the behest of the US Army.

Although no member of his staff has been willing to admit to having any working knowledge of what went on in the padded trailers used by researchers on Holmesburg property, it has since been discovered that they housed inmates undergoing chemical warfare experiments. Among prisoners, there was a circulating rumor that Kligman was "testing LSD," a drug that, in the sixties, had only started to emerge as a known hallucinogen. But records from both Woodrow Wilson's Chemical Warfare Service and the CIA's Project OFTEN, confirm that inmates were actually being given "drugs and chemical compounds" in the government's effort to identify substances that could predictably alter a person's ability to function. In fact, through a diligent Freedom of Information Act investigation, author Allen Hornblum discovered that "one of OFTEN's goals was to 'come up with a compound that could stimulate a heart attack or stroke in the targeted individual, or perhaps a new hallucinogen to cause the targeted individual to act bizarrely.'" These were, without a doubt, wartime trials.

Had Kligman been a clinical psychiatrist or a toxicologist, he certainly would have been better suited for overseeing this ethically gray research. But, as a dermatologist, he was simply unprepared for both its outcome and results.

Notes taken by Dr. Herbert Copelan, the medical director of the University of Pennsylvania's Holmesburg Prison research program, evidence the dangers posed to prisoners in these studies: "9:57 AM on 22 May 1970, . . . a 35-year-old white man, 6 feet 3 inches tall and 207.5 pounds, received an intravenous 113.2 ug. dose of Agent 926. About 30 seconds after injection, he reported nausea and slumped forward. He was immediately rolled back on the bed and his legs were elevated. He was ashen, unconscious and motionless. His skin was not moist. No radial, precordial or cervical pulsation was seen or felt. About one minutes after injection, or 15 seconds after being placed in the supine position without response, two or three precordial blows were given and regular sternal compression was started. Mouth to nose ventilation was begun some 30 seconds after the start of sternal compression."

Agent 926, also called EA 926, was a drug being tested by the US Army. As described by Dr. James Ketchum, an Army psychiatrist, "the drug defied category. It was very potent in animals because of its knockdown effect, [but] it was hard to know what effect it would have in man." Dr. Ketchum told author Hornblum that many found the drug appealing, thanks to its potential power, but these same scientists refused to work with it because it had been deemed "unsafe" by members of the Army's medical team. Despite his affiliation with the prison trials, Ketchum claimed ignorance when faced with the report that the drug was being tested on inmates at Holmesburg. He was not the only one apparently undereducated about what kinds of tests were being run out of Holmesburg: The prisoners themselves were often purposefully left in the dark.

A handful of the inmates who participated in Kligman's tests have gone on record about the trial, describing what little they knew about the operation. Certain prisoners were made to testify in front of Congress, while others have attempted to appeal to pharmaceutical companies who might be willing to pay for silence. These men speak of experiencing an intense hallucination shortly after being given a drug, which was followed by a prolonged spell of disorientation. Most inmates believe that the trial's effect has never fully left their systems. As Johnnie Williams, one prisoner, told Allen Hornblum, "I did small crimes, nonviolent crimes, things like burglary, car theft, and petty thievery . . . I had been a guy who tried to avoid arguments, but after the tests . . . I got very quick tempered and got into a lot of fights. . . . The crimes got worse . . . I went from petty thievery and busting into cars, to shootings, to assaults. I had major problems after the tests. [They] made me violent. I did things to provoke people . . . I never did that before."

No one—not even the prisoners who underwent the tests—seems to remember much about what the tests entailed. But, as Williams would later discover, Kligman did have some reservations about how his subjects would react to the experiments. It is known that, after they left their trailers and rejoined the regular prison population, they wore a badge alerting staff members, "Please excuse this inmate's behavior. He can't think or act in a coherent manner and is part of the US Army testing program." Amazingly, despite such open admission of possible psychosis, Kligman, for a time, continued this kind of testing without any interruptions or reports of concern made by lab workers, prison employees, or other administrators.

Dr. Kligman hit a major snafu in his research when, beginning in 1965, the FDA became aware that he was applying dimethyl sulfoxide (DMSO), a banned substance, on inmate's torsos. Kligman's use of a banned substance prompted the FDA to evaluate his research protocols and notes. When officials discovered the startling lack of record keeping in Kligman's lab, they announced that he was no longer an approved researcher. Kligman, though, had connections (including a lot of University of Pennsylvania officials who did not want Penn to be embarrassed), and the ban was lifted within months. However, many of the promises he made to appease the FDA, including bringing in additional, better-trained staff, never happened. Dr. Kligman's program at Holmesburg was eventually shut down in 1974, following a congressional hearing on human experimentation that created a nationwide ban prohibiting clinical trials from being run in institutions and prisons.

Approximately five years after Albert Kligman had packed up and moved his lab out of Holmesburg, his affiliation with the prison once again faced scrutiny. Following an April 1981 issue of *Corrections* magazine, which featured an article about how dioxin, a potentially toxic chemical, had been tested on prisoners during experimental trials held in Philadelphia during the mid-1960s, some Holmesburg prisoners wrote to the Environmental Protection Agency, declaring themselves part of the unlucky cohort. As a result, the EPA launched an investigation into the matter. Their determination, given over a year later, vaguely dismissed any direct correlation between prisoners' dioxin exposure and any subsequent health problems. It was a huge blow to many Holmesburg men, who were struggling not only with their history of incarceration, but also with a whole host of unexplained health problems.

The findings reeked of a cover-up, and the results were dispiriting to say the least. The *New York Times* determined that, "Somewhere almost certainly in the United States, are as many as seventy men who could help researchers determine the risks of human exposure to the poison called dioxin." When asked to weigh in on the matter, Dr. Kligman casually dismissed the inmates' concerns, remarking to the *New York Times*, "All those people could have leukemia now—about one chance in 20 billion. And I could be hit by an asteroid when I walk out on the street, but I don't think I will."

The dermatologist's brazen attitude was not just the stuff of legend: It was fact. As he grew to be both a stalwart within the University of Pennsylvania's Dermatology Department and an ethically unsound but extremely well-paid researcher, Kligman was often known to counsel young residents, "Rules don't apply to genius." Apparently neither does the Nuremberg Code.

# CHAPTER 10

## Unclear Intentions:
## Pittsburgh's Joe Magarac

Living in one of Pennsylvania's mill towns in the early 1900s, there were certain things that you could count on: If you sneezed, you'd see soot; if you worked hard, they'd work you harder; and if you died, you'd die trying. Nobody knew this better than Steve Mestrovich a local mill owner. His job was to motivate swarms of sweaty men while also maintaining his mill's safety and productivity. Beyond his professional duties, Steve also had a family to raise; most troubling was his daughter Mary who, at eighteen, was having to fend off suitors who were traveling across counties to try to win her favor. Mary was every hunky's dream, a blue-eyed, blonde woman who respected and understood the hardships of being a mill worker.

To put an end to the incessant questions about Mary's future, and to ensure that his beautiful daughter would be matched up with a deserving and righteous man, Steve announced that he would be hosting a strongman contest. Steve was so serious that he placed ads in local and nearby papers. News of the event traveled quickly and, as prospective attendance grew, Steve began to take his role of host quite seriously, even going into the city to buy kegs of beer for his guests. The rules were simple and the prize undisputable: Whoever could lift the three dolly bars Steve had brought home from his mill would win Mary's hand.

The excitement at Steve's party was palpable, as men, each burlier than the next, lined up to impress Mr. Mestrovich and, more importantly, to lay claim to Miss Mary. Each man was to lift a dolly bar that weighed 350 pounds. If he could manage that weight, he'd move on to the second bar, which was 500 pounds. The third bar threatened close to 900 pounds, and would only be attempted by the strongest of competitors.

At the end of the second round, only three men had enough mettle to pass Mestrovich's test. Luckily for Mary, her true love, the stunning Pete Pussick, happened to be among the final contestants. However, in a fate that Steve Mestrovich could likely not have foretold, the trio of men vying for his daughter all failed to lift the heaviest steel beam. Just when it seemed that all hope was lost, and that no steel worker was adequately equipped to win Mary, in strode an unmistakable stranger: Joe Magarac.

Joe Magarac, a strapping seven-foot-tall beast, commanded the attention of every single person present when he raised the nine-hundred-pound dolly bar over his head without so much as a grimace. When asked to identify himself, Magarac's last name caused a tense commotion—while it meant "donkey" or "jackass" in Croatian, no one was brave enough to laugh at this man whose strength was most certainly unmatched. And when Joe unbuttoned his shirt to expose a chest made entirely of steel, it seemed like there was nothing to do but stare. Upon further inspection, the crowd slowly surmised that it wasn't just Joe's chest that was made from steel, but his whole body! Steve Mestrovich rushed Mary to Magarac's side and explained the prize to the contest's winner; some said that Steve could barely contain his excitement over the good fortune of both his daughter and his family business.

It wasn't Mary's face—squeezed tight over the grave misfortune that had come between her and Pete—that convinced Joe to relinquish his earnings. Instead, it was Magarac's work ethic and commitment to the mills that interrupted the pending nuptials. Joe began with nary a hesitation, "I cannot marry anyone." Stopping just short of deeming Mary a distraction, Joe announced that his attention and his efforts were completely focused on his job, leaving no time to entertain or love a wife. Mary jumped into Pete's arms, and the runner-up was given the winner's prize. Magarac strode away, but not before leaving an indelible mark on the people of Western Pennsylvania.

When some steel men were pulling themselves out of bed, and others were hanging onto the edge of a bar, bleary from Imp n' Irons (from Pennsylvania's [still popular] combination of a shot of Imperial Whiskey served alongside an Iron City beer), Joe Magarac was unrested, unfazed, and unstoppable. As the story goes, having been born in an iron mine, Joe was made solidly of steel. He could be seen popping pieces of cold steel into his mouth for sustenance, and regularly drank molten steel like it was soup. Joe didn't need sleep in order to work twelve-hour shifts in the mills. He didn't need to blow off steam. And he couldn't even fathom sacrificing his talents or his goals in order to love the most beautiful woman in town.

The tale of Joe Magarac is steeped in oral tradition. For those scratching their heads, wondering why Magarac's name isn't at all familiar, consider where you were raised. While most Americans are familiar with John Henry's contributions to the railroads, Paul Bunyan's lumberjacking prowess, and Johnny Appleseed's planting acres upon acres of apple trees, the lore of a man who could log uninterrupted hours in the sometimes-suffocating steel mills is, by comparison, highly esoteric.

In the late 1800s, Western Pennsylvania mill towns like Johnstown, Morewood, Homestead, and Pittsburgh housed scores of Eastern European immigrants, some of whom had even been recruited by major mining companies to move from their homelands to the United States. Political turmoil in Europe made the mills' meager salaries—often as low as ten cents per hour—seem both stable and enticing. It was commonplace for Irish or German mill bosses to place their employees of Hungarian, Croatian, Serbian, Slovenian, and African-American descent in the depths of the mills, where the heat was high and the work backbreaking. While these men sweated, the rich local mill owners and bosses became staples in local government, known for winning over public favor by pouring money into their municipalities.

Mill workers, who were essentially itinerant laborers with no voting powers, risked becoming completely marginalized. As is noted by historian Thomas J. Misa, "Strikes, lockouts, slow times, full-scale economic depressions, and the hope of better work elsewhere resulted in a sizable 'floating population' of the least skilled, who moved on to the next mill town, to join a railroad work crew, or to sign up with a coalmine gang." The mill bosses were not ignorant to the ramifications of alienating the men who carried their companies, which leads us to the story of the Man of Steel, Joe Magarac.

Magarac was introduced in 1931 in *Scribner's Magazine* when author Owen Francis recounted tales he reportedly had learned about Joe from laborers who told, firsthand, of his prowess. From Francis, readers discovered that Joe Magarac was born abroad and later traveled to Pennsylvania to find work in a mill town. While his story mirrors the tales of so many of his countrymen-turned-colleagues, Magarac held the distinction of having been born in an iron mine, and having been made entirely of steel, a claim no other mill worker could make.

Like any humble servant, Joe Magarac seemed happy to toil in the mills, completely unrecognized for his dedication and super-human strength. But anyone who had seen him work knew that Magarac was built for bigger things. According to

Francis, Magarac's fame was initiated by his performance at Steve Mestrovich's party. However, from a more global perspective we can see that it was Francis's *Scribner* article that was truly responsible for catapulting Magarac from the depths of the mills to the forefront of the public eye.

As legend went, after Joe Magarac had become well known, mill bosses from all over Western Pennsylvania came courting, trying to lure Joe from the spot he earned working the Number Seven furnace at Mr. Mestrovich's mill. Joe wasn't leaving because he was admittedly very content; he was renting a room from Mrs. Horkey, who, perhaps because of her cooking, was known to run the best boarding house in town. In addition to this, Mestrovich gave Joe as many hours at the mill as he wanted. Joe became so proficient—sticking his bare hands into the furnace and molding steel rails with amazing accuracy—that men from the mills were known to come by and watch him work after their own shifts had ended.

With Joe's ability to make four rails in each of his hands at one time, the area around furnace Number Seven quickly became littered with stacks upon stacks of his work. He was so incredibly productive that, after time, the mill had to be temporarily closed so that demand could catch up to his supply of rails. All of a sudden the men who had lauded Magarac's work were faced with a week—maybe more—without a paycheck, all thanks to Joe's tireless work output. Steve Mestrovich was understandably conflicted, for he knew it would feel like a punishment to instruct his best worker to take some time off. However, Joe took news of the forced vacation well, admitting that he hadn't slept in something like fifteen years. So at his boss's suggestion, he agreed to spend some time away from the furnace.

When the mill reopened, the workers found their way back to their familiar posts, energized by rest and encouraged by the promise of a paycheck. But one man was missing from Mestrovich's mill: Joe Magarac. When the smelter boss went looking for Joe, he was met with a shocking sight: Magarac wasn't manning furnace Number Seven, he was in it! Standing atop a ladle that was already submerged in the molten steel, Joe announced that he never, ever, wanted to prompt the closing of the mill again. When his supervisor protested, Magarac declared that he had found a way to make Mestrovich's mill the best in Western Pennsylvania: He would, in the most literal sense, become a part of it. Magarac shouted a committed "Goodbye!" as he melted into martyrdom.

Tales of Joe's heroism grew following his death: Some stepped forward and told stories of having seen Joe rescue men from certain death, while others recounted his feats of strength that evidenced his pure dedication to the steel industry. As historian Thomas White succinctly determined, "In all of the stories, [Magarac] remained the most talented and efficient millworker anyone had ever seen. He loved making steel." Steel was the industry of the day, too. *Time* magazine in 1951 reported that "40% of all U.S. jobs depend upon steel and its users."

Frank Vittor's plaster cast for the "Joe Magarac" statue.

It is no wonder that, following Owen Francis's *Scribner* article, Magarac had been selected as the mascot for companies as large
and influential as U.S. Steel, which was worth $2,829,000,000 in
1951. He was the epitome of steel-town pride, celebrated not
only within mill culture, by also in comic books (*Joe, the Genie of*

*Steel* was first published by U.S. Steel in 1951) and by sculptors (Frank Vittor's one-hundred-foot statue of Magarac was initially slated to become the fountain at Pittsburgh's Point State Park). However, in the wake of Magarac's valiant death, many began to question the legitimacy of his legend.

For starters, when, in 1953, Hyman Richman of the *New York Folklore Quarterly* interviewed steelworkers about Magarac, many had never heard of him or his feats of strength. Upon investigation, Richman began assembling a theory that Magarac's tale was not told to Francis by proud steelworkers, but rather by greedy mill owners. As explored by academics Jennifer Gilley and Stephen Burnett, "Hyman Richman and [folklorist] Richard Dorson debunked the legend in the 1950s as 'fakelore': a figment of corporate rather than popular imagination more at home in U.S. Steel's public relations department than the immigrant mill communities from which it supposedly arose." All of a sudden Joe's tireless hours at the mill and his relentless commitment to his boss took on a nefarious light: He was the ideal steelworker, as imagined by the men whose fortunes were built on the backs of shift workers.

If skepticism prevails, we can assess that, in the midst of striking workers, financial hardships, and threats of economic depression, the corporations created Magarac, whose superhuman strength allowed him to rise above the very real grievances that labor unions had. Joe didn't need shorter hours, and would never question his wages—he was an ideal employee, much in the same way that Santa Claus is the ultimate humanitarian.

As is so often the case with legends, the true origin of Magarac's lore is lost to history. Perhaps *Scribner's* Francis was sold a bogus story by Eastern European mill workers who were happy to tell a bookish writer of this jackass of a man who was born of steel and could feel nothing outside of corporate commitment. Or, perhaps the mill bosses had created a fable to illustrate the glory given to a man willing to work as tirelessly as a mule. The truth might be tucked into a mix of these scenarios, where U.S. Steel embraced the hero of Francis's naïve article in an effort to create an indelible corporate symbol; or else, the story was erroneously credited to mill workers who had, in fact, never heard of the very man they lauded.

The legend of Joe Magarac does not necessarily have to lose its value even if his story is fakelore. As explored by Gilley and Burnett, interest in Magarac's legend made a resurgence when financial hardship fell upon the steel industry during the 1980s. When men were getting laid off, and companies were closing, tales of Joe's strength and professionalism were embraced, uniting workers in a sense of pride that was waning by no fault of their own. For if there is one thing that Western Pennsylvania will never lack, it is civic pride. In fact, such loyalty is embedded so deeply in the mill towns of Pennsylvania that it is all but impossible not to believe that there was a man who loved steel so much that he was willing to pour his heart and soul into it.

# CHAPTER 11

# Unsung Heroes:
# Pittsburgh's Polio Pioneers and
# Vaccination Research Team

All over the neighborhood, mothers sat in pairs or small groups, gossiping about dalliances and backstabbing, husbands' follies, and the butcher most likely to tip the scale in his customer's favor. But, unlike in years past, these women weren't carrying on while their children were playing under fences and along dirt roads: Their children were locked up safely inside, far from the resident monster.

Everyone had seen it: One day a child would be fine, and then without warning, he'd be running a high temperature with a case of chills that nothing could quell. That's when the panic would set in, as there was no telling what would happen when the fever broke. Sue's son just had run-of-the-mill flulike symptoms and was bouncing off the walls when he felt better. Janice's daughter wasn't as lucky: The polio virus crept into her brain stem and central nervous system, and doctors said that she'd never walk again. But neither woman would ever complain in front of Ellen, whose youngest was in an iron lung because polio had ruined his ability to breathe without assistance.

All it took was one boy or girl catching the dreaded disease. In Washington County, Pennsylvania, it was little Jimmy Sarkett who, at the age of ten, contracted the poliovirus. First he was made to stay indoors, attempting to lie still as the virus attacked his legs. The colored sign in his home's front window indicated the quarantine, announcing that neighbors and friends should steer clear of the Sarkett's stoop. Then, as was common for families of polio victims, the Sarketts were forced to ship Jimmy off to Pittsburgh, where he was checked into the Municipal Hospital for Contagious Diseases before, months later, he was moved to the D.T. Watson Home for Crippled Children in nearby Leetsdale.

No child wanted to go to D.T. Watson. All the kids there were sick, and lonely in the worst kind of way for their families. None of the patients knew why they had gotten sick, but all of them knew that they didn't want to use crutches or braces or a wheelchair for the rest of their lives. Scariest yet were the kids you'd see in the iron lung—a big, life-size tube that you were slid into so that it could help you breathe. Can you imagine climbing into a loud, humming chamber as a five-year-old, terrified that you might never be allowed out?

Polio was more than an unseen villain. Radioman Mike Silverstein described it as "the boogeyman: it was the faceless, formless menace that could come and get you." If, as a child, you couldn't understand the gravity of polio's threat, you certainly hated it for being the reason that your parents wouldn't allow you to have any fun. Asked about the various ways polio was capable of disrupting their plans, Western Pennsylvania residents John Troan, Judy Wolfington, Sidney Busis, Bernadette Baron, Ethel Bailey, Mike Silverstein, and Ronald Flynn came up with these recollections of parental panic: "We were told don't go to swimming pools, don't sit in a wet bathing suit, don't go into strange crowds, don't drink from someone else's cup, don't drink from a water fountain, don't use a telephone." The residents recalled the peculiar rumors that so often circulated, including the fear that cats were spreading the disease. In sum, because kids were discouraged from congregating in theaters, at the circus, and even at the county fair, it seemed that the common consensus was that "The summer was like, no, no, no, no, no fun!"

Polio was like a fog that held the children of American households captive or, worse yet, incapacitated them physically and emotionally. But not everyone was afraid of its crippling weight. In 1947 Jonas Salk, a young researcher raised in and around New York's five boroughs was recruited to Western Pennsylvania's University of Pittsburgh. At the time Salk was working at the University of Michigan under Tommy Francis, a New Castle, Pennslyvania, native who had made a name for himself by being the first American to isolate the human flu virus.

Salk's introduction to Pittsburgh was inauspicious to say the least. The University put Salk—who was traveling without his family on the recruiting visit—in their most esteemed residence: The University Club. At the time, the Club did not welcome Jews, although apparently no one had the guts, gall, or the stupidity to ask Salk to stay elsewhere. Left to his own devices during his stay, Salk slept with his windows open, affording him a view of Fifth Avenue and the University's esteemed Cathedral of Learning. In the morning, he awoke with his white linens covered in soot. Worse yet, when he first blew his nose, he discovered that he had been inhaling coal ash all night. In the face of the city's sideways welcome, Salk proved he was up for a challenge when he accepted the new dean of the University of Pittsburgh Medical Center's offer to start a lab in the Steel City.

Brought to "the Great Furnace of America," Salk was lured by the promise that moneyed men like Richard Mellon, Andrew Carnegie, John Weakley Chalfant, and George Westinghouse would fund his research. (For more on Westinghouse, see Chapter Twelve.) It was a high time for Pittsburgh medicine; Pitt's dean, William McEllroy, had enlisted Salk's talents around the same time that renowned pediatrician Benjamin Spock was brought to the city. Pittsburgh was on track to move from being considered "hell with the lid taken off" to a top-ten research institution funded by the National Institutes of Health.

When Salk moved his family from Ann Arbor to Lawrenceville, a working class neighborhood in Pittsburgh, he got right to work at Municipal Hospital. While Salk's commute in to work wasn't bad, the scene inside of the hospital was another story. Municipal Hospital was home to a huge polio ward, full of iron lungs and children whose bodies were wrestling with their symptoms. As a Municipal Hospital employee would later recall, "you'd hear a child crying for someone to read his mail to him or for a drink of water or why can't she move, and you couldn't be cruel enough just to pass by. It was an atmosphere of grief, terror, and helpless rage."

At the time he first began at Pitt, Jonas was still under a grant that had been funding his influenza research. Initially, his interest in polio was cursory. In fact, one of the only driving motivations for Salk to actually begin researching the virus was because it held the promise of hefty funding from the National Foundation for Infantile Paralysis (now more commonly called the March of Dimes). Salk was not alone in coveting their resources; the fight to eradicate polio was a well-funded operation that drew some of the nation's greatest virologists to spend long hours in their labs.

One year into his stay in Pittsburgh, Salk had made connections with Harry Weaver, a researcher who, due to his charisma and big-picture thinking, was tapped to create a national committee focused on polio research. Weaver offered Salk, who was considered a young and relatively inexperienced researcher, a multiyear grant in exchange for a commitment that he would work to develop a polio vaccine. All of a sudden the fact that Salk was sharing Municipal Hospital with Western Pennsylvania's polio patients was beginning to feel less and less like a coincidence.

By 1949, Salk's hospital laboratory was growing, as was his team. Regarding how he assembled his lab, writer David Oshinsky described: "Salk hired well, finding people who shared both his vision and his workaholic ways—people who could see their currently plodding tasks as the start of something special, the creation of a lifesaving new vaccine." The key players of his original team included a bacteriologist (Jim Lewis), a head technician (Byron Bennett), an animal handler (Tony Penko), and an office manager (Pittsburgh native Lorraine Friedman).

While they might have been sequestered in the basement of Municipal Hospital, Salk and his team were not operating in a vacuum. The search for a polio vaccine was a well-known project, and as a member of Weaver's national committee, Salk was in communication with scores of other research teams. Or rather, research teams were constantly in touch with the Salk lab, which was busily doing its best to determine just how many strains of the poliovirus were present in the United States. The "typing" process, tedious and repetitious, sets out to isolate and identify particular strains of a virus. While it is an essential step in understanding the makeup of a virus, typing is generally delegated to novice researchers as its success results more from patience than from skill. As a result of the Pittsburgh team's dedication to typing, some of the members of Weaver's national committee—Cincinnati's Albert Sabin, in particular—were quick to dismiss the legitimacy of Salk's lab. Sabin didn't even give Salk credit when the Pittsburgh lab was able to confirm loose speculation that polio had three distinct strains.

At around the same time as the lab's successful typing results were announced, an up-and-coming researcher, Harvard's John Enders, discovered that the poliovirus could be cultivated in test tubes, thereby eliminating the need to inject animals with the virus in order to observe its growth. The discovery was monumental, later earning Enders a Nobel Prize in Medicine and Physiology. A slowly growing national foundation of knowledge was actually beginning to support the hope that researchers could bring an end to polio. Following his discovery, Enders, who held little personal interest in studying polio, agreed to

Pittsburgh polio pioneers line up for vaccinations in the Cathedral of Learning Commons Room, February 26, 1957.

March of Dimes Foundation

provide Salk's Pittsburgh lab with tissue cultures so that they could get started with their own efforts to harvest the virus.

Despite this, Salk was hardly the front-runner in the race for the vaccine. Other teams, including one affiliated with Baltimore's Johns Hopkins University, appeared to be making headway of their own. While the common goal was certainly to find a way to eradicate polio, there was also grant money and a great amount of pride at stake, not to mention the desire to be the researching team responsible for restoring the carefree and fun nature of summertime to American children.

It is unclear just how much Pittsburgh was aware of what was going on in Municipal Hospital's basement. Sure, they saw Donna Salk and her three boys around town, especially after the family moved out to the suburbs to settle into their Western Pennsylvania life. And Jonas's name was certainly familiar, as he was gaining national notoriety as a researcher with vast potential. But the only folks who were truly aware just how stubborn Salk was, and how strenuous the pace of his work had become, were those who reported to the lab alongside of him.

Salk's crew of researchers was growing consistently, and in 1951 it welcomed three key individuals: Percival Bazeley, an Australian veterinarian who was recruited to help the Pittsburgh lab harvest the poliovirus; Julius Younger, a microbiologist with previous experience working on the Manhattan Project; and Elsie Ward, a zoologist who would serve as Younger's techni-cian. This trio of new faces was tasked with the job of growing large quantities of the poliovirus in test tubes using tissue from monkey testicles. After their initial attempts yielded too small of a result, Younger determined that using monkey's kidneys might be more productive. Younger also thought to employ trypsinization, a practice that allows a virus to be grown in large quantities.

Younger's contribution was essential, especially as the team approached its next step: preparing an "undiluted" virus that, when injected, would be "powerful enough to cause immunity and yet docile enough to do no harm." There were two significant components of this plan: First, they had to create an undiluted virus for each of the three polio strains. Second, was the fact that the team had decided not to use a live version of the virus, as was commonly believed to be the safest and most successful way to create a vaccine. Instead, the Pittsburgh lab aimed to use a recently killed virus by using samples that had been inactivated by a "cooking" process.

Although Salk presented his team's work to the twelve members of Harry Weaver's immunization committee, who wished to vote on whether tests would be run on human subjects, unbeknownst to them Jonas had already made inroads with administrators at both the D.T. Watson Home for Crippled Children and the Polk School for the Retarded and Feeble-Minded (which has since been renamed the Elwyn Institute) to test the vaccine at their facilities. While Salk was able to backdoor his fellow committee members, testing on youth populations did require cursory involvement of the National Foundation for Infantile Paralysis, as they were still funding large parts of his research. While the Foundation wanted to support the Pittsburgh lab's momentum, they also needed to protect against the possibility of any public or legal backlash. It was determined that Salk and his team could perform their tests on the children at both D.T. Watson and the Polk School, provided that they obtained parental consent "whenever possible." The very first trials were done at D.T. Watson. Because all of the patients were already infected with polio, their participation in Salk's early trials involved a much smaller risk than those institutionalized at the Polk School.

At D.T. Watson, each child was injected only with the type of poliovirus they were already carrying. Sixteen-year-old Bill Kirkpatrick was the first patient to receive the team's recent-kill virus. Kirkpatrick, who was from Wilkinsburg—a neighborhood located no more than eight miles from Municipal Hospital—had to convince his parents to allow him to participate in Salk's early trials. Kirkpatrick's recovery had been a remarkable one, taking him from being completely unable to move his limbs to his walking with the aid of canes. "The other kids were kind of frightened [of the vaccine]," he later recalled, and so it took a great deal of guts for him to be the one to "step up to bat first."

In total, forty-three volunteers at D.T. Watson were injected. Salk, who reportedly administered most of the shots, would later remark, "When you inoculate children with a polio vaccine, you don't sleep well for two or three months." Fortunately for everyone, the initial results were good: Children did not get sick, and their antibody levels were rising, evidencing that the vaccine was doing its job.

Following their success at D.T. Watson, Salk and his team traveled to the Polk School, where they completed more injections of the recent-kill virus. This was a much riskier undertaking, as none of Polk's population was infected with the poliovirus and, thanks to the many years that they had spent institutionalized, some of Polk's patients had severely underdeveloped immune systems. It is for this reason that positive results from Salk's Polk trials instilled an even greater confidence in the potential success of the team's vaccine.

The urgency of finalizing the vaccine was pressing. As the author David Oshinsky recounts, "1952 was the worst polio year on record, with more than fifty-seven thousand cases nationwide." While Salk battled with members of the committee on immunization, who, upon hearing about his team's research trials, still expressed doubt in the killed-virus vaccine, Harry Weaver began telling National Foundation for Infantile Paralysis trustees that the newest research developments were zeroing in on a much-anticipated solution. Once it became known that Weaver was talking about a potential vaccine, a *Pittsburgh Press* reporter, John Troan, who had been following the progress of his hometown team, identified Salk as the savior in question. Soon enough, word had spread far and wide, even landing Jonas in *Time* magazine during February 1952.

With the media attention came lots of pressure: from fellow researchers, from the National Foundation, from an anxious public, and from the increasing number of news outlets that were prematurely promoting Salk to a hero's status. Within a year, Salk was awarded an additional $145,000 for his continued research: His lab grew to include twenty-one full-time staff members and many more who were brought in to provide temporary assistance. Tension among lab regulars was reportedly becoming palpable, as many worried that Salk was becoming as obsessed with accolades as he was with finalizing the vaccine. However, no matter how the team was feeling about one another, they all knew that they were closing in on their shared goal.

In 1953, Jonas Salk injected his three boys with his killed-virus vaccination. Trusting in the man after whom Municipal Hospital would later be renamed, parents in and all around Pittsburgh's neighborhoods then sent their children to receive the trial vaccination. The team's confidence that they should begin national trials was based on the participation of some fifteen thousand kids from public, parochial, and private schools in and around Pittsburgh.

Henceforth known as the "polio pioneers," these kids bravely, dutifully, and in some cases completely unwillingly subjected themselves to the dreaded shot. Recalling the Pittsburgh trials, Linda Creswell-Hartman mused, "and I can remember my parents talking about should we do this, shouldn't we do it. And my father saying to my mother, 'You know what the risks are if you don't do it. What have we got to lose?' I can remember the lines going on forever. And afterwards you got warm juice . . . They were done in the gym so they had all the gym mats down, and if anybody fainted they got put on one of the gym mats for awhile." After trials were deemed successful in Western Pennsylvania, similar trials were conducted elsewhere in the United States.

On April 12, 1955, Jonas Salk traveled to attend a press conference in Ann Arbor, Michigan, where his mentor, Tommy

Francis, planned to announce the results of his field trial measuring the effectiveness of Salk's polio vaccine. The nation went into a frenzy upon hearing Francis declare, "The vaccine works. It is safe, effective, and potent." Francis went on to deem the vaccine 60 to 70 percent effective against Type I polio, and 90 percent effective against the other two types, a claim that angered Salk so much that, by the time he accepted the microphone and center stage, he used the spotlight to assail the accuracy of Francis's findings. But, what was more irresponsible than calling the vaccine 100 percent effective, was how Salk failed to thank any member of his Pittsburgh lab.

Julius Younger is the only living member of Salk's team. He moved to Pittsburgh in 1949 and found himself at home there. When the vaccine's fiftieth anniversary was celebrated in 2005, the *Pittsburgh Tribune-Review* interviewed Younger about Salk's April radio announcement, during which Salk gave no credit or acknowledgment to the members of the Municipal Hospital team. Younger admitted to feeling insulted and betrayed, recalling that, upon hearing the radio broadcast of Salk's speech, "Some of [the members of the lab] were crying . . . People really held it against him that he had grandstanded like that and really [had] done the most un-collegial thing that you can imagine."

As David Oshinsky wrote, there are "many faceless heroes of the polio crusade." There are the original members of Salk's lab; the incoming members who, like Bazeley and Younger and Ward, contributed not only hours but expertise to the research; the children of D.T. Watson and the Polk School; the Pittsburgh-area parents who believed in the vaccine; and their children who—willingly or not—availed their bodies by allowing the team to test the efficacy of the vaccine on healthy bodies.

Jonas Salk's son, Peter, addressed this issue in a speech given at the University of Pittsburgh to commemorate the fiftieth anniversary of the vaccine: "This was a Pitt vaccine . . . It was clear that the world wanted a hero, wanted a single person to be associated with something as momentous as this. But this was the work of the Pitt team: Dr. Juli Younger, Byron Bennett, Jim Lewis, Val Bazeley, the people in the laboratory, Ethel Bailey, Martha Albert—all part of that team. Everyone pulling together, contributing their skills, their expertise, their absolute devotion to get this job done and get it done quickly. . . .These people deserve such tremendous praise and thanks; so let me please thank you for what you did."

With all of those folks surrounding the Pittsburgh polio team, we have scores of unsung heroes who, collectively, helped eradicate the monster that used to terrorize the summertime of youth. As Mike Silverstein, a Pittsburgh polio pioneer declared, "This is so cool and we did it in Pittsburgh! Aren't we the best?!"

# CHAPTER 12

## *Unsung Heroes: Pittsburgh's Westinghouse Enterprise*

I t's impossible to gauge what, exactly, was going through the minds of the 1,500 people gathered in Coney Island on Sunday, January 4, 1903, when they saw Thomas Edison alongside an adult elephant. Almost certainly they were there to lay eyes on Edison, who was already known (albeit somewhat erroneously) as both the inventor of the lightbulb and the creator of the phonograph. He had widely publicized the event, hoping that his fame would draw big numbers to south Brooklyn despite the winter chill. Edison was also hoping that the spectacle would undermine the work of his competitor, George Westinghouse, thus protecting Edison Company sales.

The Luna Park Zoo had planned to put down Topsy, one of their elephants, after the beast had killed three employees in a three-year time span. True, Topsy had attacked one of her handlers after he had fed her a lit cigarette, but no matter the circumstances, zoo officials could not let three deaths be followed by a fourth. The American Society for the Prevention of Cruelty to Animals had forbidden the zoo from hanging Topsy, so Edison's offer to kill her was accepted without so much as a pause.

According to journalist Tony Long, the entire premeditated affair was smooth in its operation. In fact, zoo officials were so bent on killing Topsy that extra caution was taken to ensure her death by feeding her cyanide-laced carrots prior to Edison's show. After the crowd had assembled, "Topsy was restrained using a ship's hawser fastened on one end to a donkey engine and on the other to a post. Wooden sandals with copper electrodes were attached to her feet and a copper wire run to Edison's electric light plant, where his technicians awaited the go-ahead." Topsy didn't stand a chance against 6,600 volts, collapsing instantly. Edison made sure to educate his crowd that the elephant's death was brought to them thanks to *alternate* current. For those who missed the murder, Edison released the film, *Electrocuting an Elephant,* which, despite its grainy quality, effectively demonstrates how easy it is to kill an elephant with the use of alternating current electricity. (For those who are interested, footage of the electrocution can be found online.) Welcome to the War of the Currents.

There are no reports to suggest that George Westinghouse and his wife, Marguerite, were anywhere other than their Pittsburgh home on January 4, 1903, when Edison was putting on his murderous show. The Westinghouses had moved from New York to Western Pennsylvania in 1868; the roots that they planted were strong, tying the inventor to the city and Westinghouse's employees to their esteemed boss.

George was born in Central Bridge, New York, on October 6, 1846, and was raised in Schenectady, a village on the eastern side of the state. The second youngest of ten children born to George and Emmeline Westinghouse, George Jr. had open access to his father's machine shop when he was growing up. His dad's penchant for assigning him small chores gave George real-world exposure to the tools he would eventually use to create hundreds of patents. When George was thirteen, his father built him a workshop in the attic. He made quick use of the space, and by the time he was fifteen he had secured his first patent for an "improved grain and seed fanning or winnowing machine." Despite his prowess as an engineer, Westinghouse was not a strong student. Even though his parents wanted him to be attentive and capable in the classroom, George seemed to reserve his curiosity for the hours he spent engaged in projects of his own design.

After seeing Civil War action—first in the army, and then with the navy—at his father's behest George enrolled in Schenectady's Union College. Westinghouse spent his brief college career falling behind in his course work and fine-tuning what would turn out to be one of his most influential inventions, which offered improvements on the rotary steam engine (Patent 50,759, earned on October 31, 1865). With lousy grades and admittedly no interest in his studies, Westinghouse left what would be the last of his formal education when he withdrew from Union College after just three months of study.

Resuming his place in his father's shop, George Jr. split his attention between work his father assigned and a newfound interest in bettering train travel. During the next four years, Westinghouse created a host of inventions, all of which helped to improve the burgeoning form of transportation. His early patents include a "car replacer" to right derailed train cars; a "reversible frog"—a "segment of intersecting rail that allows one track to cross another"; and the highly influential "steam-power-brake device," which single-handedly cut down on the amount of dangerous accidents (and frustrating delays) common to train travel at that time. As his plans and projections were so focused on the railroad, it is perfectly fitting that Westinghouse met his bride, Marguerite Erskine Walker, while riding a train. The two married in 1867 and, because Westinghouse had yet to see much profit for his inventions, the newlyweds began their life under George's parents' roof.

When George was not tinkering in his workshop, he was acting as a traveling salesman, trying his best to peddle his car replacer, reversible frog, and air brake. Given his industry, West-inghouse's eventual move from New York to Pittsburgh made perfect sense. During the late nineteenth century, the Western Pennsylvania town had become "one of the nation's greatest industrial cities, notable for its glass, iron, steel, aluminum, and railroad equipment production. Cheap energy from local depos-its of bituminous coal and river and rail transportation were essential elements in its rise." In Pittsburgh, Westinghouse found easy access to affordable steel, as well as financiers who were willing to fund his projects.

By 1871, George and Marguerite had purchased a home on land where Westinghouse Park now stands in Pittsburgh's Point Breeze neighborhood. Nicknamed "Solitude," after a Catskills town near where Mrs. Westinghouse had grown up, the property included a three-story house large enough to entertain easily (as the couple was wont to do) in addition to ample land where George ran some of his experiments. As the *Pittsburgh Post-Gazette* reports, "Because Marguerite Westinghouse liked to have her husband at home, the gas wells were drilled in the back yard—four of them, beginning in 1884. Their wooden derricks towered over her flower beds and his laboratory on the estate's south lawn, along Thomas Boulevard. Westinghouse's home lab was part of the estate's two-story brick stable built in the same Second Empire style as the house; the lab's basement contained a generator and engine room for the pioneering lighting and heating systems. Wires and pipes passed through a subway tunnel to the house. There were rumors Westinghouse was conducting secret experiments there, and they were right." One of Westinghouse's most useful experiments yielded the discovery that natural gas can be accessed and piped over long distances (for both use and sale).

This is not to say that all of Westinghouse's work was done in the dark or underground—quite the contrary. Almost

Westinghouse Memorial, Schenley Park, Pittsburgh, February 2012.

immediately upon settling in Pittsburgh, he established the Westinghouse Air Brake Company; by 1881 he had formed the Union Switch and Signal Company, and by 1886 he founded the Westinghouse Electric Company. His companies employed thousands in Western Pennsylvania.

Those who encountered Westinghouse described him as anything from taciturn with a stocky build to having kind eyes and an open, warm smile. By most accounts he avoided the limelight and withheld his charm for smaller groups. As a boss, Westinghouse evoked a universal loyalty. Although he had never worked for a business other than his father's small mechanic shop, George held a very distinct understanding of how he wanted his companies to be run. By his own admission, he "tried to build up corporations which are large employers of labor, and to pay living wages, larger even than other manufacturers pay, or than the open labor market necessitates." As author Jill Jonnes notes, in addition to being one of the first American workplaces to give employees only a half-day of work on Saturdays, "Westinghouse companies would be pioneers in worker safety, disability benefits, and pensions."

By the time that George created Westinghouse Electric, he had already proven himself to be an accomplished and influential inventor. Although he would continue to apply his engineer's eye to seemingly unsolvable questions, arguably his greatest contribution to the Industrial Revolution was the work that his laborers completed while under his employ. Of his professional goals, George explained, "My ambition is to give as many persons as possible an opportunity to earn money by their own efforts." Westinghouse was in the habit of buying patents that were developed by other inventors, so that his companies were positioned to build upon the most cutting-edge products and equipment. One of the finest examples of how Westinghouse was able to successfully capitalize on other inventors' patents coincided with his getting into the business of electricity.

In the early 1880s, Thomas Edison had the electricity market cornered using direct current (DC). He had unveiled his commodification of incandescent lighting on New Year's Eve 1879 and, by 1882 the Edison Electric Company had opened its first power station, located on Manhattan's Pearl Street. Although many had contributed to the work that went into opening the power station, Edison publically celebrated being able to offer New Yorkers electricity, calling it "the biggest and most responsible thing I had ever undertaken . . . [of which] there was no parallel in the world." It was, indeed, a triumph. But many who worked with Edison did not appreciate his taking sole credit.

Meanwhile, in Pittsburgh, Westinghouse was assembling (and appropriately paying) a valuable team of inventors. One brilliant supervisory move came in 1884, when Westinghouse purchased electrical engineer William Stanley's "direct current, self-regulating dynamo" (a dynamo is a generator). Stanley's invention was groundbreaking as, before its creation, the dynamos being used by the Edison Electric Light Company to generate DC electricity were all regulated by hand.

While many in Westinghouse's position might have tried to market the invention outright, George had other ideas. Inspired by work that was being done in Europe with alternating current (AC), Westinghouse secured the US patent rights to the Gaulard-Gibbs transformer, which ran on AC. Once he had purchased an option on the rights, Westinghouse asked William Stanley to tinker with the equipment in an effort to see whether it might fit into the grand plan of the company running AC through a central power station. Thanks to Stanley's dogged work, by 1888 the Westinghouse Electric Company had an alternating current product. And, as the Westinghouse brand had already become synonymous with quality, George was able to open a central AC power station that was commercially viable despite the fact that the nation was relatively unfamiliar with this new, higher-voltage product.

The year 1888 marks the opening of Westinghouse Electric Company's Buffalo, New York, power station. That same year also marks the first time customers were introduced to the possibility of being able to choose between direct and alternating current. Additionally, 1888 was the year that saw an inventor defect from the Edison camp only to join and make great contributions to Westinghouse Electric.

Nikola Tesla is an integral figure not only in the War of the Currents, but also in the history of electricity. Having come to the United States from Croatia (by way of Paris), Tesla arrived in New York for the sole purpose of working with Thomas Edison. Described as a natural engineer—one who was so talented that he could visualize his inventions without having to conduct any literal trial and error—Tesla immediately butted heads with Edison, who believed Tesla to be a mere protégé. Thus, when Edison quieted Tesla's insistence that alternating current held greater potential than direct current (AC could be transmitted at a higher voltage, and over much longer distances), the Serbian knew that Edison would never see him as an intellectual equal.

If Tesla's autobiography is to be believed, while working under Edison he "designed twenty-four different types of machines" but, despite such productivity, Edison refused to pay a promised fifty thousand dollars for his efforts. In fact, if the story is to be trusted, Edison not only denied Tesla his earned income, but also joked off their agreement by suggesting, "You don't understand our American humor." When Edison tried to placate Tesla with a ten-cent raise, the genius quit.

Once he was a free agent, George Westinghouse sought Tesla's talents, specifically because it was Tesla who had created a rough model for an alternating current motor. When Westinghouse moved the eccentric and ingenious inventor to Pittsburgh, it lit an unstoppable rage in Thomas Edison. And, when it became obvious that Tesla's AC motor was going to propel alternating current into everyday use, Edison became even more angry: Not only did his former protégé seem happy, but he was contributing to the success of a rival company! Edison rightfully began to worry for the future of Edison Electric's fortune.

Tesla's relationship with Westinghouse Electric was relatively short-lived, as the Pittsburgh company could not afford to keep him on staff after the creation of his AC motor. In exchange for $216,600, Tesla sold his patents and left Pennsylvania with the utmost respect for those involved in his work there. Of his former employer he remarked, "George Westinghouse was, in my opinion, the only man on this globe who could take my alternating current system under the circumstances then existing and win the battle against prejudice and money power. He was one of the world's true noblemen, of whom America may well be proud and to whom humanity owes an immense debt of gratitude."

With AC customers creeping across the eastern seaboard, Edison began to wage war against Westinghouse Electric. He started with lawsuits accusing Westinghouse of patent infringement, and followed this by lobbying legislative bodies to prohibit the transmission of electricity over three hundred volts (thus rendering alternating current illegal). Neither act proved to be an effective way to thwart AC's growing presence. Following, Edison became fixated on promoting his belief that AC was much more dangerous than DC electricity. As Westinghouse Electric's customer base grew, Edison ("the Wizard of Menlo Park") began staging public electrocutions using alternating current. Having killed dogs, cats, and even a cow with AC, Edison set his sights on a much larger stage.

In 1890, two Edison employees, Harold P. Brown and Arthur Kennelly, unveiled their new invention: the first modern electric chair. In a time when lawmakers were beginning to question the brutality of death by hanging, the electric chair was presented as a more humane way to kill members of America's growing prison population. What few realized at the time was that, by funding Brown and Kennelly's invention, Edison was, in fact, pouring money into what he hoped to be his biggest anti-AC campaign yet.

Publically, both Edison and Westinghouse rejected the notion that their company's current should be responsible for the death of a prisoner. Unbeknownst to Westinghouse, however, Edison's employee Harold Brown had illegally purchased a Westinghouse AC generator, selling it to New York's Sing Sing prison along with his electric chair. In 1890, William Kemmler, the first prisoner to die by electrocution, died thanks to alternating current. The execution was reportedly an "awful spectacle, far worse than hanging," as Kemmler did not expire as a result of his first round of electricity and, after a prolonged dose of a second current, his passing left the room "smelling foul with burnt flesh." Ever the showman, Edison convinced New York papers to write that Kemmler had died not by execution or electrocution, but by "Westinghousing."

While it would be reductive to suggest that the battle between Edison's DC and Westinghouse's AC was a simple fight of evil versus good, with the benefit of history's hindsight, it does feel positive to celebrate the fact that Westinghouse Electric was able to recover from the bad publicity surrounding Kemmler's execution. In 1893, thanks to Westinghouse's tenacious sales pitch (he essentially risked making little to no profit), the Pittsburgh company won the right to light the Chicago World's Fair. It was a turning point in the War of the Currents, as is highlighted in the PBS documentary, *Tesla: Master of Lightning*: "For the twenty-seven million people who attended the fair, it was dramatically clear that the power of the future was AC. From that point forward more than 80 percent of all the electrical devices ordered in the United States were for alternating current."

George Westinghouse lived to see his alternating current triumph over Edison's insistence that DC electricity would ultimately power the United States. Westinghouse also helped to create and promote hydroelectric power as one of the nation's sources of natural energy. Although he was lauded for his foresight as an inventor, George was ultimately removed from the board of Westinghouse Electric due to concerns about his financial savvy. Westinghouse still maintained a relationship with the company he started, however, and remained staunchly revered throughout Western Pennsylvania. When he died in 1914, he held 361 patents.

While Thomas Edison might be more recognizable, Westinghouse's legacy is undeniable. In Pittsburgh he is honored with a city park bearing his name as well as a statue featuring his likeness. He is also credited for helping to form the town now known as Wilmerding, where he had built affordable company housing during the early days of Westinghouse Electric. Moreover, Westinghouse is lauded for enriching both the city's commerce and its reputation for innovation.

# SOURCES

## CHAPTER 1, UNSOLVED CRIMES: FRANKFORD'S SLASHER

Barclay, Shelly. "Unsolved Serial Murders in the United States." Historic Mysteries.com. May 28, 2010. http://historicmysteries.com/unsolved-serial-murders-in-the-united-states.

Bellamy, Patrick. "Gary Heidnik: To Hell and Back." TruTv.com. "Serial Killers: Truly Weird & Shocking." www.trutv.com/library/crime/serial_killers/weird/heidnik/index_1.html.

Davidson, Peter. *Death by Cannibal: Criminals with an Appetite for Murder.* New York: Penguin, 2006.

Gibbons, Thomas J., Jr. "Frankford Woman, 66, Found Stabbed To Death." *Philadelphia Inquirer,* November 12, 1988.

Heine, Kurt. "'Marty' Graham Guilty Of 7 Murders." *The Philadelphia Inquirer,* April 27, 1988.

Hickey, Brian. "Return to the House of Horrors." *Philadelphia Weekly,* March 13, 2002.

Hunter, Walt. "I-Team: Detectives Use New Technology To Try Solving 'Frankford Slasher' Case" CBS Philly website. December 13, 2010. http://philadelphia.cbslocal.com/video/6462083-i-team-detectives-use-new-technology-to-try-solving-frankford-slasher-case/.

———. "Police Recall 'Frankford Slasher' In Search For 'Kensington Strangler.'" CBS Philly website. December 13, 2010. http://philadelphia.cbslocal.com/2010/12/13/police-recall-frankford-slasher-in-search-for-kensington-strangler/.

James, Randy. "A Brief History of DNA Testing." *Time,* June 19, 2009.

Newton, Michael. *The Encyclopedia of Serial Killers,* 2nd ed. New York: Checkmark, 2006.

Ramsland, Katherine. "Frankford Slasher." TruTv.com. "Serial Killers: Unsolved Cases." www.trutv.com/library/crime/serial_killers/unsolved/frankford_slasher/index.html.

———. "Harrison Graham: The Corpse Collector." TruTv.com. "Serial Killers: Sexual Predators." www.trutv.com/library/crime/serial_killers/predators/harrison_graham/1_index.html.

Selway, Tim. "Frankford Yellow Jackets: 1926 NFL Champs." Pennsylvania Center for the Book. Spring 2008. http://pabook.libraries.psu.edu/ palitmap/FrankfordYellowJackets.html.

Swierczynski, Duane. "Under the El." *Philadelphia City Paper,* August 25–31, 2005.

tal. "Philadelphia Rape/Murders End." *Off Our Backs,* 17, no. 5 (May 1987):17.

## CHAPTER 2, UNSOLVED CRIMES: BELLEFONTE'S MISSING DISTRICT ATTORNEY, RAY GRICAR

Belson, Ken. "Questions on Sandusky Are Wrapped in a 2005 Mystery." *New York Times,* November 8, 2011.

Casarez, Jean. "New leads in missing Sandusky case DA." *In Session* (blog), CNN.com. November 18, 2011. http://insession.blogs.cnn.com/tag/ in-sessions-jean-casarez/.

CityData.com. "Centre County, Pennsylvania, PA" (statistics). www.city-data.com/county/Centre_County-PA.html.

Fontaine, Tom. "Jerry Sandusky charged with 40 counts related to child sex abuse." *Pittsburgh Tribune,* published on TribLive.Com, November 5, 2011. www.pittsburghlive.com/x/pittsburghtrib/news/s_765791.html.

Ganim, Sara. "Could this be Ray Gricar? Utah authorities trying to identify John Doe mystery prisoner." *The Patriot-News* published on PennLive .com, July 26, 2011. www.pennlive.com/midstate/index.ssf/2011/07/ could_this_be_ray_gricar.html.

———. "Former Centre County DA Ray Gricar's reasons for not pursuing case against Jerry Sandusky are unknown." *The Patriot-News* published on PennLive.com, November 6, 2011. www.pennlive.com/midstate/ index.ssf/2011/11/former_centre_county_da_ray_g.html.

Good, Meaghan. "Ray Frank Gricar." Posted on The Charley Project.com. July 26, 2011. www.charleyproject.org/cases/g/gricar_ray.html.

J. J. in Phila. "Sporadic Comments on Ray Gricar." CentreDaily.com (blog). www.centredaily.com/2011/03/21/2597340/main-index-32011.html.

Lohr, David. "Ray Gricar, Missing Pennsylvania DA, Opted Not To Prosecute Jerry Sandusky." *The Huffington Post,* November 11, 2011.

Martin, John P. "Six years later, district attorney's disappearance is still a mystery." *Philadelphia Inquirer,* July 31, 2011.

O'Brien, Luke. "The Mystery Of Ray Gricar, The Prosecutor Who Failed To Prosecute Jerry Sandusky (And Who Might Be Dead)." Deadspin .com. November 9, 2011. http://deadspin.com/5857966/the-mystery-of-ray-gricar-the-prosecutor-who-failed-to-prosecute-jerry-sandusky-and-who-might-be-dead.

Renner, James. "The Rivers Edge: Homicide? Suicide? Hoax? A Prosecutor Vanishes and Clues Point Everywhere at Once." *The Cleveland Times Free Paper,* 2005.

*Thirty-third State-wide Pennsylvania Grand Jury Report.* Released November 5, 2011.

Ward, Paula Reed. "$5,000 reward offered in case of missing Centre County DA." *Pittsburgh Post-Gazette.* April 22, 2005.

Weather Underground. wunderground.com.

### CHAPTER 3, UNSOLVED CRIMES: NEW CASTLE'S MURDER SWAMP

Badal, James Jessen. *In the Wake of the Butcher: Cleveland's Torso Murders.* Kent, OH: Kent State University Press, 2001.

———. Personal e-mail correspondence with the author, December 2011.

Bardsley, Marilyn. "The Cleveland Torso Murders by the Mad Butcher of Kingsbury Run." TruTv.com. www.trutv.com/library/crime/serial_killers/ unsolved/kingsbury/victim_4.html.

———. "The Kingsbury Run Murders or Cleveland Torso Murders." TruTv.com. "Serial Killers: Unsolved Cases." www.trutv.com/library/ crime/serial_killers/unsolved/kingsbury/index_1.html.

Dillinger, Vic. "The Cleveland Torso Murders." InfoBarrel.com. www .infobarrel.com/The_Cleveland_Torso_Murders.

Heaton, Michael. "Author James Jessen Badal Is Hot on the Trail of Cleveland's Torso Murders Killer." *Cleveland Plain Dealer.* Posted on Cleveland.com, August 16, 2010. www.cleveland.com/pdq/index .ssf/2010/08/author_james_jessen_badal_is_h.html.

Hiles, Joe. "New Castle, PA—Unsolved Murders." Serial Killer Central. February 20, 2006, 8:32 PM. www.skcentral.com/articles.php?article_id=488.

"Kingsbury Run." Posted on deadohio.com. (Uncredited author.) www .deadohio.com/Kinsbury.htm.

Nickel, Steven. *Torso: The Story of Eliot Ness and the Search for a Psychopathic Killer.* Winston-Salem, NC: John F. Blair, 2001: 89,170 (1939), 172.

Ramsland, Katherine. "More Haunted Crime Scenes." TruTv.com. "Notorious Murders: Timeless Classics." www.trutv.com/library/crime/notorious_murders/classics/haunted_crime_scene2/13.html.

Taylor, Troy. "Dead Men Do Tell Tales: Torso Killer—History, Hauntings & the Mad Butcher of Kingsbury Run." Posted 2004. www.prairieghosts .com/torso.html.

Wetsch, Elisabeth. "New Castle Unsolved." Crimezzz.net. 1995–2005. www.crimezzz.net/serialkillers/N/NEWCASTLE_unsolved.php.

White, Thomas. *Legends & Lore of Western Pennsylvania.* Charleston, SC: History Press, 2009.

## CHAPTER 4, UNFATHOMABLE CONDITIONS: CENTRALIA'S BURNING MINE FIRE

Bellow, Alan. "The Smoldering Ruins of Centralia." On blog, Damninteresting.com (blog). March 29, 2006. www.damninteresting .com/the-smoldering-ruins-of-centralia.

Beltz, Johnathan F. "And Yet, Centralia Still Burns Today: A Look at the Centralia Coal Mine Fire." Offroaders.com. March 13, 1998. www .offroaders.com/album/centralia/Johnathan_F_Beltz2.htm.

Commonwealth of Pennsylvania Department of Environmental Protection Bureau of Air Quality. "Centralia Mine Fire Mercury Study Final Report." March 10, 2008.

DeKok, David. *Unseen Danger: A Tragedy of People, Government, and the Centralia Mine Fire.* Philadelphia: University of Pennsylvania Press, 1986.

Guss, Jon. "Inferno: The Centralia Mine Fire." The Pennsylvania Center for the Book. Fall 2007. http://pabook.libraries.psu.edu/palitmap/CentraliaMineFire.html.

Hannon, Michael. "Anthracite Coal Strike of 1902." University of Minnesota Law Library. Undated. http://darrow.law.umn.edu/trialpdfs/Anthracite_Coal_Strike.pdf.

Jacobs, Renee. *Slow Burn : A Photo Document of Centralia, Pennsylvania.* Philadelphia, PA: University of Pennsylvania Press, 1986.

Johnson, Deryl B. *Centralia.* Mount Pleasant, SC: Arcadia Publishing, 2004.

Kitsko, Jeffrey J. "Centralia Mine Fire." On blog, pahighways.com. www .pahighways.com/features/centralia.html.

Klebon, Joe. "The Centralia Mine Fire." On blog, http://centraliaminefire .weebly.com.

Krajick, Kevin. "Fire in the Hole: Raging in mines from Pennsylvania to China, coal fires threaten towns, poison air and water, and add to global warming." Smithsonianmag.com. Posted May 2005. www .smithsonianmag.com/travel/firehole.html.

Roberts, Peter. "Anthracite Coal Communities: A Study of the Demography, the Social, Educational and Moral Life of the Anthracite Regions." 1904.

Rubinkam, Michael. "Pa. Coal Town Above Mine Fire Claims Massive Fraud." Associated Press. March 9, 2010.

Quigley, Joan. *The Day the Earth Caved In: An American Mining Tragedy.* New York: NY, Random House. 2007.

### CHAPTER 5, UNFATHOMABLE CONDITIONS: PHILADELPHIA'S TELEPORTATION EXPERIMENT

Bielek, Alfred. Speech given at the Mufon Conference, Dallas Texas, January 13, 1990. Transcribed by Clay Tippen, October 12, 1991. Posted on www.softwareartist.com.

———. "Alfred Bielek: The Philadelphia Experiment and Montauk Survivor Accounts." www.bielek.com/ab_albielek.htm.

"Brother Carlos Allende: Holy Observer of the Philadelphia Experiment." (uncredited author.) Brotherhoods-Secret Societies website. www .bibliotecapleyades.net/bb/allende.htm.

Elliott, S. M. "Hoaxes from Space: The Philadelphia Experiment Part I." *Swallowing the Camel* (blog). November 10, 2009. http:// swallowingthecamel.blogspot.com/2009/11/hoaxes-from-space-philadelphia.html.

Frazier, Jim. "Mystery Man Offers Death Bed Statement: Riddle of Carlos Allende Resolved." *THE NEWS* of Colorado Centennial Country, August 22, 1986: 1, 8.

"*History's Mysteries:* True Story of The Philadelphia Experiment." Film produced by Weller Grossman, aired on A&E Television Networks. DVD release date: July 14, 2008.

Hochheimer, Andrew H. www.softwareartist.com/philexp.html.

———. Transcript from Fox 50's "SIGHTINGS" Show. Air Date: September 4, 1992.

"The 'Philadelphia Experiment.'" Department of the Navy—Naval History and Heritage Command. November 28, 2000. www.history.navy.mil/faqs/faq21-1.htm.

Schuessler, John F. "A Brief History of MUFON." www.mufon.com/.

## CHAPTER 6, UNFATHOMABLE CONDITIONS: PHILADELPHIA'S EASTERN STATE PENITENTIARY

Browne, James P. *Phrenology: and Its Application to Education, Insanity, and Prison Discipline.* London: Bickers & Sons, 1869.

Cassidy, Michael. *Prison and Convicts. Remarks from Observation and Experience Gained during Thirty-seven Years Continuous Service in the Administration of the Eastern State Penitentiary, Pennsylvania.* Philadelphia: Patterson & White, 1897.

Dickens, Charles. *American Notes.* Reprint, London: Penguin, 2002.

Dolan, Francis X. *Eastern State Penitentiary.* Charleston, SC: Arcadia Publishing, 2007.

*Eastern State Penitentiary Bulletin Collection,* January 29, 1955.

*Ghost Hunters,* Season 2, Episode 10, "Return to Eastern State." Executive Producers: Craig Piligian, Tom Thayer. Pilgrim Films & Television Inc. Aired September 28, 2005.

Gilfoyle, Timothy. *A Pickpocket's Tale: The Underworld of Nineteenth Century New York.* New York: Norton, 2006.

Harding, Robert. Letter to George Thompson, Esq., 1843.

"History of Eastern State Penitentiary, Philadelphia." Posted on EasternState.org. (no author credited). www.easternstate.org/learn/research-library/history.

Kahan, Paul. *Eastern State Penitentiary: A History.* Charleston, SC: History Press, 2008.

"The Penitentiary Revelation," *Philadelphia Inquirer,* May 1, 1877: 1.

Philadelphia Society for Alleviating the Miseries of Public Prisons, *Extracts and Remarks on the Subject of Punishment and Reformation of Criminals.* Philadelphia, PA: Zachariah Poulson, 1790.

"Prison Labor," *Philadelphia Inquirer,* June 7, 1877: 1.

Tassin, Susan Hutchinson. *Pennsylvania Ghost Towns: Uncovering the Hidden Past.* Mechanisburg, PA: Stackpole Books, 2007.

Wines, Frederick Howard. "The Problem of Crime," *Charities Review* 7 (October 1897).

## CHAPTER 7, UNFINISHED BUSINESS: SCHUYLKILL'S MOLLY MAGUIRES

Albright, Charles; Francis Wade Hughes; R. A. West. *The Great Mollie Maguire Trials.* Pottsville, PA: Chronicle Book and Job Rooms, 1876.

Aurand, Harold. *Molly Maguires to the United Mine Workers: The Social Ecology of an Industrial Union, 1869–1897.* Philadelphia: Temple University, 1971.

Broehl, Wayne G. *The Molly Maguires.* Cambridge: Harvard University Press, 1964.

Campbell, Patrick. *Who Killed Franklin Gowen?* P H Campbell (self-published), 2002.

Dewees, Francis Percival. *The Molly Maguires: The Origin, Growth, and Character of the Organization.* B. Franklin, 1877.

Geringer, Joseph. "Allan Pinkerton and His Detective Agency: We Never Sleep." TruTv.com. "Gangster & Outlaws: Cops & Other Characters." www.trutv.com/library/crime/gangsters_outlaws/cops_others/pinkerton/1.html.

Hannon, Michael. "Anthracite Coal Strike of 1902." University of Minnesota Law Library. Undated. http://darrow.law.umn.edu/trialpdfs/Anthracite_Coal_Strike.pdf.

Kenny, Kevin. *Making Sense of the Molly Maguires.* New York: Oxford University Press, 1998.

Linder, Douglas O. "The Molly Maguires Trials: An Account." Posted on the University of Missouri-Kansas City Law School, 2010. http://law2.umkc.edu/faculty/projects/ftrials/maguires/mollytrialaccount.html.

Morse Jr., John T. *American Law Review,* Jan., 1877: 233. Qtd. in Rhodes.

Pinkerton, Allan. *The Molly Maguires and the Detectives.* New York: G.W. Dillingham, 1905.

"The Reign of Law." *New York Times,* September 8, 1875.

Rhodes, James Ford. *History of the United States of America: From the Compromise of 1850 to the McKinley-Bryan Campaign of 1896, Vol 8: 1877–1896,* Chap. 2. New York: Macmillan, 1919.

"Trial of Molly Maguires." *The New York Times,* May 13, 1876.

Weisman, Peter A. *The Molly Maguires* (1970). For Lehigh University, 1999, as posted at: www.lehigh.edu/~ineng/paw/paw-history.htm.

Woodiwiss, Michael. *Organized Crime and American Power: A History.* Toronto: University of Toronto Press, 2001.

### CHAPTER 8, UNFINISHED BUSINESS: LANCASTER'S PAXTON BOYS

Barber, Rhoda. *The Paxton Boys Remembered taken from Recollections Written in 1830 of Life in Lancaster County 1726–1782 and a History of Settlement at Wright's Ferry, on Susquehanna River.* The Historical Society of Pennsylvania with the Balch Institute for Ethnic Studies.

Brubaker, Jack. "An Indian Account of Conestoga Massacre: It Happened in Church." Lancasteronline.com. August 30, 2005.

———. *Massacre of the Conestogas: On the Trail of the Paxton Boys in Lancaster County.* Charlestown, SC: The History Press, 2010.

Cavaioli, Frank J. "A Profile of the Paxton Boys: Murderers of the Conestoga Indians." *Lancaster County History Society Journal,* 87 (1983): 74–96.

Clare, I. S. *General History of Lancaster,* chap. 1. Lancaster, PA: D. S. Stauffer, 1892.

"The Conestoga Massacre." Author Unknown. NativeAmericanNations .com. www.nanations.com/dishonor/conestoga-massacre.htm.

Dunbar, John Raine, Ed. *The Paxton Papers.* The Hague: Martinus Nijhoff, 1957.

Eshleman, Henry Frank. *Lancaster County Indians: Annals of the Susquehannocks and Other Indian Tribes of the Susquehanna Territory from about the Year 1500 to 1763, the Date of Their Extinction. An Exhaustive and Interesting Series of Historical Papers Descriptive of Lancaster County's Indians Prior to and during the Advent of the Paleface.* Oakland, CA: Express Print Co., 1909.

Franklin, Benjamin. "An Account of the Paxton Boys' Murder of the Conestoga Indians, 1764." Posted on ExplorePAhistory.com. http://explorepahistory.com/odocument.php?docId=1-4-26.

Frost, John. *Border Wars of the West: Comprising the Frontier Wars of Pennsylvania, Virginia, Kentucky, Ohio, Indiana, Illinois, Tennessee, and Wisconsin; and Embracing Individual Adventures Among the Indians, and Exploits of Boone, Kenton, Clark, Logan, Brady, Poe, Morgan, the Whetzels, and Other Border Heroes of the West.* Internet Archive digital edition. 2009. http://archive.org/details/borderwarsofwest00fros.

Hindle, Brooke. "The March of the Paxton Boys." *William and Mary Quarterly*, 3rd Series 3 (October, 1946): 467.

Historical Society of Pennsylvania. "The Insurrection of the Paxton Boys (1860)." www.archive.org/details/insurrectionofpa00hist. Accessed through Open Library.

Jacobs, Wilbur R. *The Paxton Riots and the Frontier Theory.* Chicago: Rand McNally, 1967.

Kenny, Kevin. *Peaceable Kingdom Lost: The Paxton Boys and the Destruction of William Penn's Holy Experiment.* New York: Oxford University Press, 2009.

Kirk, Andrew. "Desperation, Zeal, and Murder: The Paxton Boys." Penn State University's Pennsylvania Center for the Book. Fall 2009. http://pabook.libraries.psu.edu/palitmap/PaxtonBoys.html.

Knight, Peter. *Conspiracy Theories in American History: An Encyclopedia, Volume 1.* Santa Barbara, CA: ABC-CLIO, 2003.

Mancini, Alexandra. "The Paxton Boys and the Pamphlet Frenzy: Politics, Religion, and Social Structure in Eighteenth-Century Pennsylvania." www.publication.Villanova.edu/Concept/2007/07_papers_html/Mancini-Paxtonboy.

Nestor, William R. *"Haughty Conquerors": Amherst and the Great Indian Uprising of 1763.* Santa Barbara, CA: Greenwood Publishing, 2000.

Pencak, William and Daniel K Richter. *Friends and Enemies in Penn's Woods: Indians, Colonists, and the Racial Construction of Pennsylvania.* University Park, PA: Penn State Press, 2004.

*Pennsylvania Archives.* First Series, Vol. IX: 748–759.

Proud, Robert. *The History of Pennsylvania, in North America, from the Original Institution and Settlement of that Province, under the first Proprietor and Governor Williams Penn, in 1681, till after the Year 1742*

*. . . To Which is Added a Brief Description of the Said Province and of the General State, in Which it Flourished, Principally Between the Years 1760 and 1770.* 2 vols. 1797–1798. Spartanburg, SC: Reprint Co., 1967.

Roberts, Kenneth. *Arundel.* Camden, ME: Down East Books, 1995.

Rothbard, Murray N. *Conceived in Liberty.* Auburn, AL: Ludwig von Mises Institute, 1999.

Smith, Matthew and James Gibson. *A Declaration and Remonstrance of the Distressed and Bleeding Frontier Inhabitants of the Province of Pennsylvania.* 1764.

Spencer, Jesse Ames. *The United States: Its Beginnings, Progress and Modern Development,* vol. 2. Pasadena: American Educational Alliance, 1912.

Stokes, James. Lancaster County Historian. E-mail correspondence with the author: November 14–18, 2011.

Tully, Alan. *William Penn's Legacy: Politics and Social Structure in Provincial Pennsylvania, 1726–1755.* Baltimore: Johns Hopkins University Press, 1977, 1974.

Waldrep, Christopher and Michael A. Bellesiles, *Documenting American Violence: A Sourcebook.* New York: Oxford University Press, 2006.

## CHAPTER 9, UNCLEAR INTENTIONS: PHILADELPHIA'S DR. ALBERT KLIGMAN

Albarelli Jr., H. P. "'Human Guinea Pigs' Demand Justice." WorldNetDaily .com. Posted on May 30, 2002.

Beerman, Herman and Lazarus, Gerald. *The Tradition of Excellence: Dermatology at the University of Pennsylvania, 1870–1985.* Philadelphia: University of Pennsylvania Press, 1986.

Blivaiss, Naomi. "Decades-Old Prison Tests Stir Controversy." *Daily Pennsylvanian,* November 19, 1998.

CIA memorandum to Inspector General. May 6, 1974: 3. Qtd. in Hornblum.

Davis, Alan J. "Sexual Assaults in the Philadelphia Prison System and Sheriff's Vans." *Trans-Action* 6 (1968): 8–16.

Draelos, Zoe Diana, MD. "The Future of Cosmeceuticals: An Interview with Albert Kligman, MD, PhD." *Dermatol Surg* 31, no. 7 Part 2, July 2005.

Gellene, Denise. "Dr. Albert M. Kligman, Dermatologist, Dies at 93." *New York Times,* February 22, 2010.

Hillman, Susan. "Using Prisoners for Medical Research." *The Examiner,* February 6, 2011.

*The Hippocratic Oath.* Translation from the Greek by Ludwig Edelstein. From *The Hippocratic Oath: Text, Translation, and Interpretation,* by Ludwig Edelstein. Baltimore: Johns Hopkins Press, 1943.

Hornblum, Allen M. *Acres of Skin: Human Experiments at Holmesburg Prison, A True Story of Abuse and Exploitation in the Name of Medical Science.* New York, NY: Routledge, 1998.

———. Hornblum's interview with Margaret Grey Wood, February 17, 1997.

———. Hornblum's interview with Jack Lopinson, March 14, 1994.

Hutton, Herbert J. Memorandum and order issued on 26 June 2011. Concerning Civil case: Yusuf Abdulaziz, et al. v. City of Philadelphia, et al.

"'In Prison Air': Echoes of Life Behind Bars." *Day to Day,* National Public Radio broadcast, hosted by Madeleine Brand. December 21, 2005.

"Investigating the Investigator." *Time,* August 5, 1966.

Jaschik, Scott. "Sentenced to Science." InsideHigherEd.com. November 8, 2007. www.insidehighered.com/news/2007/11/08/hornblum.

Name Withheld. Letter to the EPA. January 12, 1981 Qtd.in Hornblum.

Reiter, Keramet. "Experimentation on Prisoners: Persistent Dilemmas in Rights and Regulations." *California Law Review,* 2009.

Robbins, William. "Dioxin Tests Conducted in 60s on 70 Philadelphia Inmates, Now Unknown." *New York Times,* July 17, 1983.

Sidman, Jessica. "Swollen Feet and a Wanted Apology: Controversy Renewed with New Book about Penn Experiments." *The Daily Pennsylvanian,* November 8, 2007.

Tyson, Peter. "The Hippocratic Oath Today." *NOVA* via pbs.org. Posted on March 27, 2001.

Urbina, Ian. "Panel Suggests Using Inmates in Drug Trials." *New York Times,* August 13, 2006.

Washington, Harriet A. *Medical Apartheid: The Dark History of Medical Experimentation on Black Americans from Colonial Times to the Present.* New York: Random House Digital: Jan 8, 2008.

## CHAPTER 10, UNCLEAR INTENTIONS: PITTSBURGH'S JOE MAGARAC

Blair, Walter. *Tall Tale America: A Legendary History of Our Humorous Heroes.* Chicago: University of Chicago Press, 1987.

Botkin, Benjamin Albert. *The American People: Stories, Legends, Tales, Traditions, and Songs.* Piscataway, NJ: Transaction Publishers, 1946: 80–89.

Curran, Ann. "A Search for Our Symbol: Defining Pittsburgh in Visual Terms Has Been a Challenge. A Look at Some Ideas: Past, Present and Future." *Pittsburgh Magazine,* October 2009.

Gilley, Jennifer and Stephen Burnett. "Deconstructing and Reconstructing Pittsburgh's Man of Steel: Reading Joe Magarac Against the Context of the 20th-Century Steel Industry." *Journal of American Folklore,* vol. 11, 1998.

Misa, Thomas J., with contributions by Charles Hardy III and Dan Cupper. "Chapter 2: Steel City and Mill Towns." ExplorePAhistory .2011. http://explorepahistory.com/story.php?storyId=1-9-15&chapter=2.

Misko, Stephanie. "Pennsylvania Folklore . . . or is it Fakelore?" Pennsylvania Center for the Book. Fall 2008. http://pabook.libraries.psu .edu/palitmap/JoeMagarac.html.

"STEEL: Out of the Crucible" *Time,* November 12, 1951.

White, Thomas. *Legends & Lore of Western Pennsylvania.* Charleston, SC: History Press, 2009.


## CHAPTER 11, UNSUNG HEROES: PITTSBURGH'S POLIO PIONEERS AND VACCINATION RESEARCH TEAM

Benison, Saul. *Tom Rivers—Reflections on a Life in Medicine and Science.* Cambridge, MA: 1967.

Byers, Stephen J.; Dennis Cohen; et al. *Defeat of an Enemy: University of Pittsburgh Remembering Polio Celebration.* Pittsburgh: University of Pittsburgh Press, Reed & Witting Company, 2005.

Carter, Richard. *Breakthrough:The Saga of Jonas Salk.* Cronulla, Australia: Trident Press, 1966.

"Closing in on Polio," *Time,* March 29, 1954.

Edners, John F., Frederick C. Robbins, and Thomas Weller. "The Cultivation of the Poliomyelitis Viruses in Tissue Culture." Nobel lecture, December 11, 1954.

Fabregas, Luis and Jennifer Bails. "Younger Proud to be a Part of History, Still Angered by Salk's Slight." *Pittsburgh Tribune-Review,* April 3, 2005.

Glazier, William. "The Great Furnace of America," in *Pittsburgh,* ed. Roy Lubove, 1976: 23.

Lubove, Roy. *Twentieth-century Pittsburgh: Government, Business, and Environmental Change.* Pittsburgh: University of Pittsburgh Press, 1996: 196. Qtd. in Oshinsky.

Markel, Howard, MD, PhD. "April 12, 1955—Tommy Francis and the Salk Vaccine." *N Engl J Med* 352, no.14 (April 7, 2005).

Oshinsky, David M. *Polio: An American Story.* New York: Oxford University Press, 2005.

Perry, Pamela. "Polio: Enemy of Youth." *Inquiry* at Indiana University, Indiana University Foundation, Bloomington, Indiana, Winter 1979–80.

*Polio DVD 827,* UPTV Interviews. English Rm. 1. Filmed April 10, 2005. Transferred to DVD on January 18, 2007. Transcribed by Hughes.

*Polio DVD 823.* Filmed April 10, 2005. Transcribed by Brant.

Rinaldo Jr., Charles R., PhD. "Passive Immunization Against Poliomyelitis: The Hammon Gamma Globulin Field Trials, 1951–1953." *American Journal of Public Health* 95, no. 5 (May 2005): 790–799.

Salk, Jonas to Dr. W. S. McEllroy, December 9, 1947, Box 4, Folder 7, Salk Papers.

Seeman, Bruce Taylor. "The shot felt 'round the world." *The Seattle Times,* April 10, 2005.

Shors, Teri. *Understanding Viruses.* Sudbury, MA: Jones & Bartlett Learning, 2009.

*The Shot Felt 'Round The World.* Directed by Tjardus Greidanus. Steeltown Entertainment Project, 2010. Documentary.

Srikameswaran, Anita. "Polio pioneer: A Wilkinsburg Teen Was the First to Get the Trial Vaccine." *Pittsburgh Post-Gazette,* July 2, 2002.

"Trypsinization of Adherent Cells." Johns Hopkins University. SOP NUMBER: 114, GRCF: THE CELL CENTER. Revised 6/02.

University of Pittsburgh School of Medicine Fast Facts. www.upmc.com/mediarelations.

Weber, Michael. *Don't Call Me Boss: David L. Lawrence, Pittsburgh's Renaissance Mayor,* 1988, 202–3; Qtd. in Oshinsky.

Wilson, John R. *The Margin of Safety: The Story of the Poliomyelitis Vaccine.* London: Collins, 1963: 77.

Younger, Julius. Unpublished Memoir, 5–7. Qtd. in Oshinsky.


CHAPTER 12, UNSUNG HEROES: PITTSBURGH'S WESTINGHOUSE ENTERPRISE
Bussler, Mark. *Westinghouse: The Life & Times of An American Icon.* Produced by Inecom Entertainment Company, 2010.

Byllesby, H. M., Letter to the Editor, *Electrical Engineer* (August 1888): 367.

Cheney, Margaret. *Tesla, Man Out of Time.* Englewood Cliffs, NJ: Prentice-Hall, 1981.

"History of Research & Technology." Posted on Westinghousenuclear.com. www.westinghousenuclear.com/our_company/Research_&_Technology/history_research_technology.shtm.

Hounshell, David. "Pittsburgh: A Brief History." Posted on the University of Virginia's HistoryofTechnology.org. www.historyoftechnology.org/pittsburgh/pittsburgh_history.html.

Jonnes, Jill. *Empires of Light: Edison, Tesla, Westinghouse, and the Race to Electrify the World.* New York: Random House, 2003.

King, Gilbert. "Edison vs. Westinghouse: A Shocking Rivalry." *Past Imperfect* (blog), *Smithsonian* website. Posted on October 11, 2011. http://blogs.smithsonianmag.com/history/2011/10/edison-vs-westinghouse-a-shocking-rivalry/.

Kupper, Dan. "George Westinghouse Historical Marker." Posted on ExplorePAhistory.com. 2011. http://explorepahistory.com/hmarker.php?markerId=1-A-1A9.

Leupp, Francis E. *George Westinghouse: His Life and Achievements.* Boston: Little, Brown, 1918.

Long, Tony. "Jan. 4, 1903: Edison Fries an Elephant to Prove His Point." Wired.com. Posted on 4 January 2008.

Lowry, Patricia. "Vanished Westinghouse Estate Here Yields Some Secrets." *Pittsburgh Post-Gazette,* May 2, 2006.

Moran, Richard. *Executioner's Current: Thomas Edison, George Westinghouse, and the Invention of the Electric Chair.* New York: Borzoi Book, published by Alfred A. Knopf, 2002.

Ravage, Barbara. *George Westinghouse: A Genius for Invention.* Austin, TX: Steck-Vaughn Company, 1997.

Reis, Ed. "Early Westinghouse Robots Were Fascinating Characters." *Pittsburgh Engineer Magazine,* 2005.

———. Radio broadcast. Recorded by KDKA and posted at the Heinz History Center: www.heinzhistorycenter.org/secondary.aspx?id=209.

———. "An Industrialist for the Ages." *Society for the Advancement of Education.* May, 2011.

———. "A Man for His People: The Stature of George Westinghouse as an Engineer Is Rivaled by His Skill and Integrity as a Leader." *The American Society of Mechanical Engineers,* October 2008.

Schatz, Ronald W. *The Electrical Workers: A History of Labor at General Electric and Westinghouse, 1923–60.* Champaign, IL: University of Illinois Press, 1987.

Skrabec, Jr., Quentin R. *George Westinghouse: Gentle Genius.* New York: Algora Publishing, 2007.

Tesla, Nikola. *My Inventions.* First published in *Electrical Experimenter,* 1919.

*Thirty Years of New York, 1882–1912: Being a History of Electrical Development in Manhattan and the Bronx.* New York: Press of the New York Edison Company, 1913.

Uth, Robert and Margaret Cheney. "Nikola Tesla: Life and Legacy." Related to the PBS Documentary, *Tesla: Master of Lightning.* PBS.org. Posted on April 2004.

Wogan, David. "The Westinghouse/Edison Rivalry—Stray Dogs, Circus Elephants, and Getting 'Westinghoused.'" *Plugged In* (blog), Scientific American website. December 5, 2011.

# INDEX

# ABOUT THE AUTHOR

**Kara Hughes** was born and raised a Buckeye, but now calls Brooklyn home. She graduated with a BA from Harvard University and earned an MFA from the University of Pittsburgh. She holds a number of jobs, including teaching and writing; her first book, *Speaking Ill of the Dead: Jerks in New York History,* was published in 2011 by Globe Pequot Press.